The American Social Experience Series

GENERAL EDITOR: JAMES KIRBY MARTIN

EDITORS: PAULA S. FASS, STEVEN H. MINTZ,

CARL PRINCE, JAMES W. REED & PETER N. STEARNS

LIBERTY, VIRTUE, AND PROGRESS

*Northerners and Their War
for the Union*

EARL J. HESS

NEW YORK UNIVERSITY PRESS
NEW YORK AND LONDON
1988

Library of Congress Cataloging-in-Publication Data

Hess, Earl J.
Liberty, virtue, and progress.
(American social experience series ; 10)
Includes index.
1. United States—History—Civil War, 1861–1865—
Social aspects. 2. United States—Politics and
government—Civil War, 1861–1865. I. Title. II. Series.
E468.9.H57 1988   973.7   88-1620
ISBN 0-8147-3451-0

New York University Press books are Smyth-sewn and printed
on permanent and durable acid-free paper.

Contents

Contents

Acknowledgments

This book began as a dissertation for the American Studies Committee at Purdue University. Work for the completion of the dissertation was facilitated by two David Ross Grants, in 1984–85 and 1985–86, from the Graduate School of Purdue University. Further financial support came from the American Studies Program and the History Department at Purdue University. All of this support was not only gratefully accepted but essential to the completion of the work. In addition, an Advanced Research Grant from the U.S. Army Military History Institute, Carlisle Barracks, Pennsylvania, greatly aided in the final stages of research.

The members of my dissertation committee, Lester H. Cohen and Robert E. May of the Department of History and Leonard Neufeldt of the Department of English, provided thoughtful evaluations of the work, which aided in its improvement. Other individuals who offered me their advice and personal encouragement at the dissertation stage included Darlene Clark Hine of the Department of History, John H. Thompson of Oklahoma Christian College, Oklahoma City, Dennis L. Noble of Port Angeles, Washington, and Richard J. Sommers, Archivist-Historian of the U.S. Army Military History Institute.

I also wish to thank several individuals who read the manuscript and kindly offered helpful suggestions for turning it into a book. They include: John J. Contreni, head of the Department of History, Purdue

University; James M. McPherson of Princeton University; George M. Fredrickson, Edgar E. Robinson Professor of United States History, Stanford University; Reid Mitchell of Princeton University; and Charles W. Royster, T. Harry Williams Professor of American History, Louisiana State University.

It is almost a truism that the dissertation director is the individual singled out for special acknowledgment. The major professor usually bears the brunt of his student's follies, flights of fancy, triumphs, and tragedies. In this case, I can assert that Harold D. Woodman has borne his share. In addition to chairing the American Studies Committee, teaching, and working on major research projects of his own, he always had time to discuss whatever was on my mind. His scholarly ability, patience, dedication to his profession, and his personal kindness to one who needed all these things in a mentor were greatly admired and appreciated. His example taught me not only what a historian should do in the classroom and when formulating a research project, but how a scholar should act in all facets of his profession. I hope that the extent to which this work offers something worthy to the scholarly community will serve as a testimony to his skill as an educator and historian and to his personal commitment to achievement.

Introduction

This study grew from a desire to understand how a society emotionally conducts a long, costly war effort. I wanted to discover what factors motivated Northerners to support the war to save the Union and then to sustain their war effort in the face of the unexpectedly high cost in battlefield suffering. After reading numerous personal sources from both soldiers and civilians, it became clear that ideas and cultural values played a highly significant role. I argue strongly for ideology and culture as major—if not key—motivations for any society engaged in a war that is large enough to demand the support of a majority of its citizens. I concentrate on one society and one war effort to illustrate this generalization.

The cultural values that motivated Northern society and the ideas that were connected with those values were at the basis of American identity. Self-government, democracy, individualism, egalitarianism, and self-control did not necessarily complete the list of cultural values underlying the Northern war effort, but they were the values most consistently discussed by a wide variety of people in and out of uniform. These values were the common property of the Northern people; they were instrumental in promoting a consensus and provided a commonly understood language that served to explain the Southern rebellion and why it was important for Unionists to crush it. War was an enterprise containing forces that could tear a people apart just as easily as draw them together. Ideology possessed great potential for halting the disintegration of purpose. Ideas that were basic to the very definition of American nationalism were reasserted; the war forced Northerners to rethink their sometimes automatic allegiance to them, conclude they were still valuable, and use them to justify their war effort.

Even as ideology brought people together, it worked to separate them when battlefield defeat and a realization of the tremendous effort needed to defeat the Confederacy became apparent. By the summer of 1862, a fracture between those Northerners who supported new, more radical policies to prosecute the war and those who could not condone such measures as conscription, confiscation of private property, and the emancipation of slaves began to turn the Northern war effort into one of the most divisive in American history. Those who protested such policies retained their belief in the fundamental cause for prosecuting the war; their devotion to the Union and the ideal of self-government remained strong. But they feared the new measures might weaken or destroy liberty in the North, and they framed their objections in ideological terms. Dissenters were in the awkward position of opposing the means while continuing to support the ends of the war. The dissenters' harassed plea for common faith in their definition of American values will be discussed, but the vigorous prosecutors of the Union war effort—those who supported the new policies and justified them through ideology—are the main subjects of this study.

To sustain a major conflict such as the Civil War, even dissenting Northerners had to assert their belief in the principles of their national existence. Rather than being guided by events, Northerners made a conscious decision to pursue and sustain their effort to save the Union. A sense of purpose, a clear belief in the value of their cause, and a strident faith in their own ability to suffer without losing either of those things brought Northerners through the most difficult war America has fought.

Clearly, it was the people who sustained the war for the Union. Notions concerning the cultural values and ideas that were connected with the war effort were pondered and commented upon in diaries, letters, and memoirs. The expressions of educated, thoughtful citizens were important in my understanding of the role played by these values, but the common people were given equal consideration. War offers the historian every opportunity to discover the thoughts of commoners, for it forces people to work through the reasons for disrupting their lives and gambling with their futures. In the case of the Civil War, America's costliest conflict, we have an abundance of published and unpublished personal accounts, which are the foundation of this study.

A strong sense of moral purpose underlay the Northern war effort, and perhaps it is safe to say that that type of purpose is essential to sustain any major war effort. Northerners believed that the conflict was a grand struggle to preserve free government in North America, a struggle which had implications for the preservation of political freedom in the world at large. When they also came to realize that slavery had to die along with the Confederacy, yet another self-satisfying moralistic element was added to their conception of what the war meant. Robert Penn Warren described this as a "treasury of virtue" accummulated in Northern consciousness that served as a bank account of morally righteous attitudes toward what had been accomplished by the Confederacy's defeat.[1] This treasury has long since been emptied. Today the Civil War seems to be little more than a historical pageant portrayed in hackneyed formulas on television miniseries. The myth of the Lost Cause, through romanticizing what was destroyed by the North, has sapped the war for the Union of its moralistic implications. This study is an effort to recapture a sense of that heady experience when people throughout the North were convinced that the fate of ideals depended upon the success of their war effort.

CHAPTER I

Freedom and Self-Government

Only three weeks after his country split apart and went to war with itself, a Cincinnati editor tried to compare the opposing values at stake.

On one side is arrayed the doctrine of Secession—with its inevitable consequences of disintegration, disorder, lawlessness, public robbery, and repudiation of all obligations, public and private: on the other, is arrayed the Constitutional Government of the country, with its adjuncts of public order, obedience to law, security to property, and fidelity to all obligations. On the one side is an established and beneficent government, resting on the democratic principle of the will of the majority; on the other, is a disorganizing usurpation, resting on the ambition of a political faction, and deriving no authority whatever from the people. On the one side, is a free Constitution, consecrated by the patriot fathers of the Republic, and approved by seventy years of successful trial; on the other, is an odious innovation, hatched by a band of conspirators at Montgomery, whose chief end is the perpetuation and extension of human slavery. On the one side, is a government hitherto obeyed at home, and respected abroad; on the other is an upstart oligarchy, reluctantly submitted to within its own borders, and justly despised by every foreign power. On the one side, the struggle is unequivocally one for the rights of the people; on the other, it is just as plainly one for the supremacy of a slave propaganda.[1]

This editor, to a significant extent, encapsulated the issues of the war and expressed them in terms that his readers would have had little trouble understanding. Contained in this quote are references to the rebellion as involving a contest between democracy on the Northern side and tyranny on the Southern side. Slavery, the basis of the Confederacy, constituted the power base of the aristocracy that had destroyed free government in the South through its accumulation of power. With the firing on Fort Sumter, the conspiracy of the slave power attempted to spread its system of black bondage and white political slavery to the North. The attack on Sumter, which represented an attempt to control the whole nation and not just the South, represented the most serious breakdown of law and order the nation had ever witnessed. Thus, order versus chaos, democracy versus tyranny, the virtue needed for self-government versus the selfishness that made tyranny possible were all wrapped up in the very definition of the Southern rebellion.

From the very beginning, Northerners made use of the language and values available to them in order to make sense of the rebellion. This process branded the South as the antithesis of what Northerners believed their country stood for. The process of defining the national crisis also assured Northerners that their region retained a firm grasp on those values that made America unique. The sides were being formed in the collective and individual minds of the North; lines were being drawn in those first confusing months of the war, and issues were condensing into guide posts for belief and motivation for action. A consensus in favor of war against the rebellion was swiftly formed.

One of the most important values that came to be associated with the war effort in Northern minds was individualism. As a concept it was new, having been first discussed at length by the French observer Alexis de Tocqueville when he visited America in the 1830s. "Every individual is always supposed to be as well informed," Tocqueville wrote in *Democracy in America*, "as virtuous, and as strong as any of his fellow citizens." This feeling bred a strong belief in the autonomy of the citizen, no matter how lowly in station. Only if his actions harmed the equal right of his fellow was the individual to be hindered by forces larger than himself. No laws, social organizations, or governmental interference were called for as long as the citizen respected the rights of all, while he enjoyed his own. While on the public level the individual had certain obligations to society—to obey the law, to contribute to mutual defense, to participate honestly in the political life of the people—he had no obligations to anyone but himself on the private level. As Tocqueville put it, the individual "is the best and sole judge of his own private interest."[2]

There certainly existed at least the potential for an aggressive kind of individualism in mid-nineteenth-century America. Once recognizing the right for personal development, the citizen would be hard pressed to keep his demands to a minimum. The Union soldier and novelist Albion Tourgee wrote that the "individual clamors for self-direction, equality of right, of privilege, of opportunity." But just as certainly there were limits to self-development. Although rich by the standards of most of the rest of the world, mid-nineteenth-century America was still an economy of relative scarcity. There were no large, nationally based corporations, no assembly lines producing huge amounts of consumer goods, or a large white-collar working force. Most Americans lived a modest life of subsistence working on farms, in factories, or in small shops. Wealth and happiness—as in all eras and nations— were difficult to achieve. All society could realistically offer the hard-working individual was the freedom to choose a mode of livelihood, to dispose of the results of his labor, and to have a say in the running of government. Individualism did not mean real control over one's life but the opportunity to attempt it. Thus, Northerners praised their nation for supporting an individual's basic need to feel in control of his destiny. "There is no other country in the world," asserted Mortimer D. Leggett, a civilian general of the Union army, "that affords such facilities and inducements for developing individuality, manly independence and ready adaptability to surrounding circumstances, and no other where the individual man stands out so distinctively as an institution by himself."[3]

Because the focus was on the individual, not on a class, egalitarianism became equally important in the definition of America. Even as they de-emphasized class distinction, Northerners strove to show they were not social levelers. They sought to equalize the opportunities for distinction based on merit. Those individuals who were able to advance more rapidly in the financial, political, and social world did so not because of artificial advantages, such as inherited wealth or class legislation. It was important to believe that the American system was one in which intelligence, hard work, and a bit of luck merited one's rise. Northerners were not concerned with inequalities of wealth or social station, as long as the system of equal opportunity was operating to prevent rigid class lines. There was little to fear from a system in which the lowly could rise and the high could fall.[4]

The egalitarian ideal was most appropriate to a society of middle- and working-class citizens. George Sidney Camp, who wrote one of the most incisive and clear-headed treatises on American society to appear in the antebellum period, pointed out that a principle such as equality was plain and simple; it was thus easily accepted by everyone. It was the simplicity of such values that made manifest the "character-istics of truth and justice" in them.[5]

The values associated with the American brand of democracy played a large role in Northern conceptions of the rebellion. Latent during the colonial period, the concept of democracy gained wide currency during the turmoil of the Revolution and the Confederation period. From that point on, and particularly with the advent of Jeffersonian republicanism in 1800 and the triumph of Jacksonianism in the 1830s, a distinctively egalitarian twist was added to the concept of democracy. In America, it became impossible to separate equality from democ-racy. Not only would the latter word denote a system of self-govern-ment, but it would also imply a social commitment to equality of opportunity among individuals in all other areas as well. The right of the citizen to participate in politics, for example, would be equal to the right to participate in the economic opportunities offered by the na-tion.[6]

Abraham Lincoln was probably the most important spokesman for democracy in America during the Civil War. The conflict was fought to preserve, in his words, "that form, and substance of government, whose leading object is, to elevate the condition of man—to lift artifi-cial weights from all shoulders—to clear the paths of laudable pursuit for all—to afford all, an unfettered start, and a fair chance, in the race of life." Like his fellow Northerners, Lincoln automatically connected political democracy, embodied in the government, with opportunity in nonpolitical areas as well.[7]

Democracy, egalitarianism, and individualism were all part of the middle- and working-class culture of mid-nineteenth-century America. The middle ranks of society were generally viewed as the backbone of the nation. Known variously as " 'the people at large,' the whole

community, the Nation, the commonality, the generality," the benefits
and responsibilities of democracy, egalitarianism, and individualism
rested on their shoulders. As the historian and Jacksonian Democrat
George Bancroft noted, it was a stable foundation. "The multitude is
neither rash nor fickle. . . . The people is firm and tranquil in its
movements, and necessarily acts with moderation, because it becomes
but slowly impregnated with new ideas." Conservatism of this type
was reinforced by offering to individuals a system based on the maxi-
mum use of their most coveted possessions. Andrew Carnegie, who
came to America before the war and who tried years later to explain to
Europeans what made America tick, offered an insight into why so
many immigrants crowded the nation's entry ports.

They have developed in the United States into one of the most conservative
communities in the world; conservative of their powerful government, of their
Supreme Court and of their Senate, and of all that makes for the security of
civil and religious liberty, of the rights of property and the constitutional right
of each individual citizen to the pursuit of happiness in his own way.

Americans tried to preserve their self-interest, thought Bancroft, by
retaining what they cherished "as the most precious of possessions"—
self-government.[8]

This was not mere rhetoric. For mid-century Northerners, self-
government was a living ideal. They were acutely conscious of the role
America played in what many of them referred to as a grand experiment to see if a people could govern itself. There was a theoretical as
well as a practical level to discussions about self-government. Northerners spoke of self-government as a glittering possibility whose practical evolution was being worked out right in their own country. It
became solidly identified with the most basic definition of America.

The rebirth of self-government, after its brief moments in ancient
Greece and Rome and its long absence since, coincided with the
creation of America. The concept of republicanism, originating from
many points and periods of time but reaching its peak in Anglo-
American politics of the eighteenth century, helped to explain the
theory of self-government. It posited an inevitable opposition between
the governed and the ruler. Power, the domain of the ruler, had an
inherent tendency to encroach on liberty, the domain of the governed.

Given this fact of political life, the best form of government, it was thought, was one controlled by the people themselves. But man's nature, which made him susceptible to the temptation always found in power, posed a threat to the working of free government. Tyranny, or the excessive use of power, resulted when individuals in government abused liberty by transgressing the bounds of power assigned them. Anarchy, or the absence of government, resulted when the people themselves abandoned moral restraint and worked for the good of themselves as individuals or as cliques rather than for the good of the whole, thus abusing the delicate nature of free government.[9]

This was a fear of all who believed in political freedom: how to maintain the balance between a government strong enough to perform the duties of government but not strong enough to destroy freedom. Conversely, how far was one to trust the masses with power, short of endangering political and social stability? Republicans of the eighteenth century argued that the only way was to rely on the virtue of the people. If citizens recognized the need to safeguard both liberty and a sufficiently strong government, self-government would be possible. If they had the moral stamina to maintain the balance between power and civic responsibility, self-government would be assured. When the founding fathers wrote the Constitution, their faith in the wisdom and virtue of the people had been shaken by the confusion and social unrest of the Confederation period. The result was the system of checks and balances that became the foundation of American governance. They believed that if the people were not trustworthy then government itself had to have built-in safeguards against popular abuse, even as the people governed themselves.[10]

By the 1860s a host of other cultural influences had taken hold in America to weaken formal republican theory,[11] but the general ideas of self-government did not disappear. The war raised anew questions historically asked of self-government in America. Northerners asked if their character was adequate for the maintenance of free government, which was the formal, institutionalized form of liberty. They asked if their cultural traits of individualism, democracy, and egalitarianism threatened or supported self-government. They wondered if individually and collectively they had the required self-control to preserve freedom.

Historically, one of the most serious threats to virtue was prosperity. The temptation to acquire personal fortune was viewed by earlier republicans as a threat to the welfare of the community.[12] A constant theme throughout the commentary of the Civil War generations was the question of whether or not prewar prosperity had sapped the sense of civic responsibility needed to maintain the collective experiment of self-government.

Virtue, then, was still seen by the time of the Civil War as a significant trait in a free people. Members of the war generations were not naive about man's nature. As General John Logan put it, a problem as old as man himself had been to "live together in obedience to the better instincts of humanity and to repress the selfishness, avarice, ambition, injustice of the nature" of man. Logan saw it as an opposition of "individual ambition against the prerogatives, rights, and interests of mankind in general."[13]

Yet, while they mused about the inherent clash of good and evil, Northerners also asserted their faith that good, on the whole, would win out. They had to assert this if they wanted to believe in the perpetuity of self-government.[14] In an essay written in 1854, George Bancroft strove to explain how man's capacity for good inevitably led to the continuous progress of humanity. Improvement came about due to a constant interaction of each man's peculiar, individual characteristics and the possibility inherent in all men for achieving "the ideal man."[15]

Every one . . . perpetually feels the contrast between his own limited nature and the better life of which he conceives. He cannot state a proposition respecting a finite object, but it includes also a reference to the infinite. He cannot form a judgement, but it combines ideal truth and partial error, and, as a consequence, sets in action the antagonism between the true and the perfect on the one side, and the false and the imperfect on the other.

Bancroft saw the struggle of sordid self and ideal model as boding well for the future of free government.

Virtue was a faith for many who believed in the possibility of free government, but it was also a concept that was abused as much as it was honored. Contemporary observers noted that it played a utilitarian role in America. Alexis de Tocqueville defined this as the "principle of self-interest rightly understood," which made individual and collective interests co-dependent.

In the United States hardly anybody talks of the beauty of virtue, but they maintain that virtue is useful and prove it every day. The American moralists do not profess that men ought to sacrifice themselves for their fellow creatures *because* it is noble to make such sacrifices, but they boldly aver that such sacrifices are as necessary to him who imposes them upon himself as to him for whose sake they are made.

Self-interest was an inevitable human motive, and Americans tried to harness it for the common good. "They therefore do not deny that every man may follow his own interest, but they endeavor to prove that it is the interest of every man to be virtuous." Because government was the only way to insure equal justice for all, each citizen viewed "the fortune of the public as his own, and he labors for the good of the state, not merely from a sense of pride or duty, but from what I venture to term cupidity." [16]

The American George Sidney Camp offered a more subtle insight into self-government. He argued that moral resolution—not moral action—was the key to preserving freedom. It was not necessary that the citizen be virtuous in his acts, but only that he have within him the capacity for resolving to do good. This resolution was coupled with self-interest to lead him toward virtuous actions when he practiced self-government. "Republican government does not rely upon the state of the public morals," Camp insisted, "but upon the union of the virtuous impulses of a moral nature with the strong motives of a personal interest." Since "we feel that our private interest is entirely implicated in the public weal," the result was a self-interested drive harnessed for the enjoyment of public liberty. [17]

In short, virtuous citizens guarded liberty not out of altruism but out of a knowledge that the best way to safeguard their individual interests was to safeguard their common interests. "Americans believe their freedom to be the best instrument and surest safeguard of their welfare," Tocqueville observed. "They are attached to the one by the other. . . . They believe . . . that their chief business is to secure for themselves a government which will allow them to acquire the things they covet and which will not debar them from the peaceful enjoyment of those possessions which they have already acquired." Americans readily identified the loss of their property as one result of the collapse of free government. An American, Joseph Thompson, stated bluntly how this self-interest guaranteed the citizen's loyalty to his nation. "A man's family, his shop, his farm, are so many hostages for his loyalty to a state that is constituted upon the very principle of protecting him in their possession and use."[18]

Self-government then was a system, according to Northerners, in which the average citizen had a very real and personal stake. In addition to being spiritually roused by the idea of self-government, an ideal sought by so many people in many lands, the citizen could also realize the practical benefits of maintaining a system of governance in which he could have a say, in order to insure the safety of his possessions. American nationalism, self-government, and property were all part of the same package.

The identification of the government and freedom became nearly complete when people referred to "free institutions," a rather archaic phrase to our ears but one that was reiterated constantly by members of the Civil War generations. Its parameters of meaning were wide and were flexible enough to include nearly any social fixture that seemed to cement allegiance to the idea of free government and to the American nation. Yet, it was also a set of very specific, concrete services that Northerners cherished. They vowed to regard institutions as "sacred trusts" and often reeled off long lists of them. Their form of government headed the lists. According to former Ohio lawyer and general M. D. Leggett, others included: "our common schools, colleges and universities; our postal facilities, telegraphs and railroads; our caucuses, town meetings and conventions; our debating clubs, stump-speaking and newspapers; our ballot-boxes and legislative assemblies; our workshops and farms and real estate tenures." They were threads binding all citizens in a mixture of self-interest and national pride. Northerners believed that these institutions grew from and begat the American character, supporting such traits as individuality, adaptability, and morality.[19]

The government, the educational system, free-enterprise capitalism, and a host of other American features institutionalized liberty. They were liberty's bulwarks; if they were allowed to weaken into disuse or crumble under the pressure of outside aggression, there was no hope for freedom. To guard against either possibility, Americans sought to keep the idea of liberty uppermost in the nation's collective imagination. Taught in the schools, marketed by the popular-culture industry, reinforced by sentiment and symbolism, the concept of freedom suffused American life. Tocqueville observed that "republican notions insinuate themselves into all the ideas, opinions, and habits of the Americans." Northerners in particular believed that education and literacy were tools of civic virtue. They worked hard to improve both public education and higher levels of learning in order to produce good citizens. Textbooks were filled with ideological lessons, including the need to balance selfish needs with the common good. If children did not learn the lesson in school, they were also exposed to it in the popular juvenile press.[20]

The popular-culture industry reinforced these values. By the 1860s, Beadle's very popular dime-novel series included forty-two books on the Revolutionary War, which so often appeared as the penultimate expression of civic virtue. Statues and prints of George Washington portrayed him as the supreme symbol of the Revolution and all it implied in terms of positive character. The deluge of fiction, nonfiction, and literature written about Washington reiterated this theme. Americans were surrounded by evidence of the virtuous nature of their culture.[21]

Ironically, Northerners were not the only Americans exposed to the teachings of this ideology. Much historiographical debate has been waged about the distinctiveness of Southern culture. Certainly, with the onset of the rebellion, Northerners came to believe that basic differences separated their section from the South. But their perceptions were highly motivated ideologically, and Northerners were under tremendous pressure after Fort Sumter to justify their war on the Confederacy. While the idea of cultural distinctiveness was a great aid in encouraging support for the war, it seems less than convincing in hindsight. The American ideology that motivated Northerners was the common property of all Americans; the average Southerner was also a capitalist, a believer in the concept of self-government, individualism, egalitarianism, and democracy. The only significant difference between the North and the South was the existence of black slavery, for it supported a minority strain of the American creed that lacked regard for democracy and egalitarianism and promoted a vision of self-government that was based on racial inequality and social hierarchy. Although a minority view, this strain and the social institution that supported it colored Northern perception of the South, making it difficult for Northerners—even if they had wanted to—to see the average Southerner as anything but enslaved by power-mad slaveholders.

Those who advocated a system of governance based on social inequality included many wealthy planters, social theorists, politicians, clergymen, newspaper editors and correspondents, intellectuals, and writers. Decrying what they termed "unlimited Republicanism," they strongly distinguished between a republic and a democracy. They believed democratic practices had destroyed the checks and balances built into the republican system, which were designed to avoid excesses of the popular will. False faith in the "reason" of man and consequent belief in universal suffrage were the culprits. Southern hierarchists reminded Northerners that Adam was given the opportunity to prove his self-control in Eden and failed miserably. "Man is not capable of self-government," asserted Stephen Elliott, a Savannah clergyman, "because he is a fallen creature, and interest, passion, ambition, lust, sway him far more than reason or honor." If man was indeed capable of self-control, there would be no need for government at all. But the continued existence of governmental authority proved the continued failure of man to reproduce Eden.[22]

Hierarchists believed that the principles upon which Northern government was based had to be changed. Mass democracy was not only unnecessary but dangerous for a republic. Northerners had to give up "any faith in man's virtuous self-government," according to Stephen Elliott, "any idea that society or government can exist without due classification." Hierarchical republicans stressed subordination, defined as "the obedience and the reverence of duty" of one to another, not inferiority, which they defined as degradation. "Without this discrimination between subordination and inferiority," continued Elliott, "there can be no highly civilized society. It is the support of all authority, the true moral principle of all order in social life."[23]

Hierarchists were obsessed with social stability and believed the best way to achieve it was through rigidity of class. B. N. Palmer of

South Carolina argued that the lack of distinct classes in the North explained the fanaticism of that section. Certainly, individuals in the North held the views required to stabilize society; but they were isolated, unable to form a class "holding the balance of power in the nation." Only the South retained the necessary social stratification for control of the masses. "We are the land of rulers," asserted a Georgian patrician, "fanaticism has no home here." A North Carolinian rejoiced that Southern domestic institutions indoctrinated all to accept the fact that "those who shall rule shall be always prepared to control those under them." [24]

But the mainstream of Southern society was affected by influences other than a strident belief in social heirarchy. Modern, opportunistic values entered Southern consciousness wherever the economy offered people the chance for advancement. Upcountry yeomen, low-country farmers, merchants, and industrialists embraced capitalism with vigor. To a large extent, as hierarchist Stephen Elliott noted, the areas exposed to influences from outside the south were most likely to fall victim to such heathen ideas. [25]

Even small slaveholders were opportunists. The expansion of the cotton market convinced them to leave behind paternalism for commercial gain. They believed in the individual and in upward social and geographic mobility, while the hierarchical vision of paternalists came from, among other things, their long settlement in the same area. Opportunistic slaveholders were distinct from these stable, wealthy planters. They bought and sold black property as a market investment, moved west to enhance their opportunities, entered and left the slave-holding ranks and re-entered them again when they had the money to buy more slaves. Their progressive, modern attitude identified them as exemplars of "the southern version of the American creed." [26]

The mainstream South and the hierarchists were tied by slavery in a bond that motivated all Southerners to fight for their independence. Southerners were united in their desire to keep the black in a low, degraded status, for that racial separation provided the base for the social status of even the poorest white man. "The presence of the black race in America," wrote Andrew Jackson Donelson of Tennessee, had "enabled the white man to treat as his equal all of his own race." Black slavery was, in essence, what made white equality possible in the minds of the mainstream South. Hierarchists agreed with this view-point. As B. M. Palmer put it, "It matters not whether slaves be actually owned by many or by few, it is enough that one simply belongs to the superior and ruling race, to secure consideration and respect. So that . . . all the political benefit which springs from the existence of such an order, lodges with the entire population who have any control over the land."[27]

A second way in which the South was united by slavery was politi-cal in nature. The institution of slavery represented even to nonslave-holders a test of self-determination and of property rights. Viewed as a local institution, whose legalization was reserved by the Constitution to state governments, slavery acted as a bellwether of the degree to which Northerners and the federal government respected local sover-eignty in the South. It was placed on the same level as ownership of other property, such as livestock, land, and produce. If denied the right to own slaves, Southerners could not help but view their other property rights as threatened. David Hubbard, an Alabama congress-man, spelled it out in 1851: "It is clear that the power to dictate what sort of property the State may allow a citizen to own and work—whether oxen, horses or negroes . . . on account of its morality, is alike despotic and tyrannical, whether such power is obtained by conquest in battle or by a majority vote."[28]

Northerners were unable or unwilling to acknowledge the somewhat complicated Southern ideological scene. They tended to brand the entire South by its most radical visionaries and ignored evidence of the existence of an ideology among mainstream Southerners that was sim-ilar to their own. When Northerners commented on Confederate vice-president Alexander Stephens's famous "Cornerstone Speech" of 1861, for example, all they could see in it was Stephens's assertion that the "great physical, philosophical, and moral truth" of the South was that blacks were an inferior race and needed to be enslaved. Stephens was no hierarchist; in the same speech he went on to assert that whites were equal before the law. But in Northern eyes, black slavery branded the South as a land of despotism. In formulating a mind-set geared toward prosecuting a major war, there was no room for subtle under-standing of the Southern scene. Abraham Lincoln clearly expressed how his section viewed the Southern definition of liberty. Ignoring the

mainstream concern for white equality, he told an audience at Baltimore's Sanitary Fair in 1864:[29]

> . . . but in using the same *word* we do not all mean the same *thing*. With
> some the word liberty may mean for each man to do as he pleases with himself,
> and the product of his labor; while with others the same word may mean for
> some men to do as they please with other men, and the product of other men's
> labor. Here are two, not only different, but incompatible things, called by the
> same name—liberty.

Using the cultural values available to them, Northerners interpreted
the war against the Southern rebellion in terms of national character.
The conflict would be the supreme test of that character and the
commitment of the Northern people to freedom. Did they have the
wisdom to recognize fundamental issues at stake in the war; did they
have the virtue to put their health and lives on the line to support the
conflict on the battlelines and at home? Did they have the self-control
to endure horrifying and new experiences, keeping the issues and goals
of the war in focus, and to win the struggle? Finally, did they have the
lasting strength to keep their war for the Union alive in their own and
the collective memory of their country, despite the passage of time and
the coming of a new era in America that would threaten some of the
values fought for on the battlefield?

CHAPTER 2

The Nation's Crisis

With the breakup of the Union, Northerners became acutely aware of comparisons between the nation's crisis and the struggle their forefathers endured to create the American experiment. According to Oliver Wendell Holmes, Sr., time seemed no longer a barrier to the past. "We cannot fail to observe how the mind brings together the scenes of to-day and those of the old Revolution. We shut up eighty years into each other like the joints of a pocket-telescope." The crisis of 1861 also seemed to be the crisis of America's accumulated past. Members of the Civil War generations felt a responsibility to preceding Americans and to those of the future. "We are trustees of the life of three generations," Holmes continued, "for the benefit of all that are yet to be."[1]

Parallels with the events and attitudes of the revolutionary generation were evident. Northerners firmly believed, as their ancestors had believed of the British, that a conspiracy existed among Southern slaveholders. This fear began long before secession, but it seemed to be confirmed by the events of the 1860s. Although the conspiracy idea originated among a small group of abolitionists during the thirty years before, it gained widespread currency with the repeal of the Missouri Compromise in 1854. By the time of the *Dred Scott* decision, many in the upper section believed the conspiracy aimed to spread slavery into the North, using the slave owner's legal right to transport chattel through free territory as an excuse. Many antebellum Northerners viewed the slave-owning clique as dominating all aspects of Southern life.[2]

During the Civil War, Northerners believed that the result of this conspiracy was secession and the creation of a Southern confederacy. Seneca Thrall, an Iowa surgeon in Grant's army, referred to the Confederate leaders as "ambitious, aspiring, unprincipled politicians." People generally recognized that the Rebels were led by conniving slave owners, having created a "conspiracy of Cotton Aristocrats," as the wife of a Union naval officer put it. Politicians, planters, and military figures cooperated in a "compact of violence, fraud and treachery" that took the South out of the Union.[3]

Northerners commonly viewed the rebellion as "unnatural." This remark stemmed not from a philosophical hatred of war but from the nature of the Southern confederacy. A conspiracy of wealthy slave-holders, who had suppressed democracy in the prewar South, seemed to have engineered secession. In contrast to the Northern government, the Confederacy was unnatural because it lacked a widespread, democratic base of support among the people. Northerners widely believed that the nation could have been spared a bloody war except for the designs of a clique.[4]

Not surprisingly, many saw the cause of this unnatural combination as money. "How sad it seems," lamented Nathan Webb, an enlisted man in the 1st Maine Cavalry, "that unholy ambition, and love of filthy lucre wrung from the blood of another race" had brought the nation to war. Maria Lydig Daly, an Irish immigrant who was married to a New York City judge, curtly wrote that the only divinity Southerners saw in their divine institution was profit. It was a popular notion that Southerners aimed in the rebellion for a higher level of material wealth than they already had achieved.[5]

The belief of some Northerners that a desire for profit motivated the Rebels was a recognition of the South's power base. Northerners came to realize that slavery had so suffused Southern institutions as to explain everything about that section. Soldiers gathered from their experiences in the South that slavery and a landed aristocracy were twins. J. W. Price, a Kentucky infantryman, fully recognized slavery's woeful impact on whites. It "not only enslaves the blacks, but it bows down the poor whites with a yoke more gauling [sic], while it ruins the rich by enabling them to lead a life of indolent ease." The suppression of free speech, free inquiry, and free education led to destruction of republican rights. This was recognized by many, including Ohio artilleryman John Stahl Peterson. "A cringing servility must be generated and maintained on the one side," Peterson asserted, "and a haughty and exacting superciliousness on the other."[6]

It was natural that a society based on slavery should seek a government based on that institution. Walt Whitman recognized this is an 1856 essay (unpublished during his lifetime), in which he argued that Southerners believed a republic could not be sustained by a free people. The safest haven for a republic was a society based on bondage. Northerners of lesser talents agreed with Whitman. W. H. Price, an officer abroad the USS *Albatross*, looked back to John C. Calhoun to prove that Southerners had long believed that democracy engendered social anarchy in the North, while the steady social foundation of slavery provided order and stability. Northerners clearly saw that the Southern system was either latently or actively opposed to their own. The rebellion represented "merely the development *[sic]* of the philosophy of slavery against citizen suffrage," according to Alton, Illinois, businessman Moses Atwood, "the *right* of the majority to rule, and freedom of expression."[7]

But the Confederacy resulted from more than a passive acceptance of slavery by Southerners. Henry Alden, a direct descendant of the Pilgrim John Alden, compared the sectional troubles to tensions between ancient Sparta and Athens. It was not "the simple fact of human slavery," he thought, that had brought on war between the two antagonists, "but slavery made indispensable as a *peculiar institution*, as an organized fact, as a fundamental social necessity." In short, Southerners had come to embrace the institution, to make of it a distinctive feature of their society. Thus, it *"must* come into conflict with the totally opposite institutions of democracy, and that not because it is merely or nominally slavery, but because it is a political organ modifying the entire structure of government." The logical conclusion was, as a Pennsylvania captain put it, that *"Human Bondage* is the corner stone of the so-called Southern Confederacy."[8]

Northerners viewed the Confederacy as a despotism. Even before fighting broke out, lawyer George Templeton Strong of New York predicted the nature of Southern political life to come.

Democratic theories of universal suffrage and the Rights of the People stand no chance against resolute men who have attained power and mean to keep it in times of revolutionary excitement. If the Southern Confederates hold together long enough to take definite political form, their government will be that of a strong, unscrupulous aristocracy. Malcontents will be promptly silenced or hanged, and even the sacred fundamental constitutional right of secession will not be exercised without serious danger and embarassment.

Similar judgments were echoed by many other Northerners. Ransom Bedell, a private in the 39th Illinois Infantry who felt strongly enough about the war to write a lengthy essay on slavery and the nature of the Confederacy, spoke in terms of despotic government. "An exclusive Class, an irresponsible aristocracy, claim the right to use and appropriate a whole Nation for their own ends, pleasure, power, and proffit [sic]."[9]

This created an odd political situation. "In a monarchical form of government," wrote Indiana soldier Jacob Power, "fighting for Liberty is justifiable. But in a free government, fighting for a Despotism is certainly the most ridiculous thing on record." Many Northerners believed that Southerners revelled in the principles that were antithetical to their own. Lydia Maria Child, who was a popular author, Transcendentalist, and advocate of women's rights, could only conclude that the Rebels saw positive ends in what were clearly evil notions. "They *do* dislike governments based on ideas of freedom and equality. They *like* despotism, and they *believe* in despotic principles." Ralph Waldo Emerson expressed it well when he wrote: "The Southerner says with double meaning, 'Cotton is King' . . . intimating that the art of command is the talent of their country. We reply, 'Very likely, but we prefer a republic.' "[10]

In the same sense that their ancestors had viewed Britain immediately before and during the Revolution, Northerners saw Southerners as having lost their grip on true republican principles. Wealth, taken from the hands of enslaved blacks, had corrupted Southern society. Slaveholders had managed to control all aspects of Southern life before 1861, including political institutions. Secession was simply a confirmation of this scenario, as the slaveholding conspiracy attempted to further tighten its grip on the lower section of the country by establishing national independence.

Yet, the mere existence of this evil was not sufficient to bring sectional war to America, just as the mere existence of corruption and conspiracy in Britain was not enough to spark a revolution against the mother nation. In both cases, the perception of a direct attempt by the corrupted member of the commonwealth to subvert the liberty of the healthy member was the spark needed to impel action. In the eighteenth century, it was the attempt to impose stricter imperial control on the colonies. In the nineteenth century, it was an act of violence designed to break a standoff between the authority of the old government and the sovereignty of the new Southern government. When Confederate batteries shelled Fort Sumter, it seemed to Northerners a direct attack on the whole governmental system established by the founding fathers for the protection and prosperity of America.

Ironically, the secession of seven Southern states in the winter of 1860–61 did not produce undivided Northern alarm about the preservation of free government. Secession did not inevitably lead to war or to threats directed at freedom in the North. Some commentators still pictured liberty as viable, despite the breakoff of half the nation's territory. They recognized that freedom was dead in the South but affirmed its health in their section. Ohio lawyer Rutherford Hayes argued that his section could easily constitute a great nation by itself. "Twenty millions in the temperate zone," he reasoned in his diary, "stretching from the Atlantic to the Pacific, full of vigor, industry, inventive genius, educated, and moral; increasing by immigration rapidly, and, above all, free—all free—will form a confederacy of twenty States scarcely inferior in real power to the unfortunate Union of thirty-three States which we had on the first of November." For Hayes, the freedom of the healthy member was in no danger, as long as the sectional issue remained a process of peaceful separation.[11]

Hayes represented one extreme reaction to the stunning fact of secession that winter and early spring. Other Northerners responded with hot-headed rhetoric about the need to maintain the Union at all costs; but most people were too surprised, confused, or disheartened by the nation's breakup to know what should be done about it. Neither

President Buchanan nor Lincoln provided clear and strong leadership, as the public remained largely uncommitted to a united course of action.[12]

The firing on Fort Sumter on April 12, 1861, changed all that. It refocused the sectional debate and created a mighty consensus in favor of war. Northerners were shocked that their Southern neighbors resorted to violence in a situation that could have been solved by nonviolent means. Southerners stepped outside the framework of laws and government that regulated acts of passion against the commonwealth by choosing to settle the question of United-States-versus-Confederate sovereignty in Charleston Harbor by a resort to arms. Francis Wayland, New Haven lawyer and later a Yale professor, stated it clearly in an *Atlantic Monthly* article.[13]

. . . and it must be remembered that education and habit had trained us to an implicit reliance on the sufficiency of our laws and the competency of our Constitution to meet and decide every issue that could possibly be presented. We could conceive of no public wrongs which could not be redressed by an appeal to the ballot-box, and of no private injuries for which our statutes did not provide a suitable remedy.

Northerners spoke of law as an intimate part of self-government. Men participated in free government in order to insure equal opportunity for all individuals. "Laws are merely the *resolutions* of community to abide by and enforce the principles of justice," according to George Sidney Camp.[14] They were highly important symbols of a person's or a people's moral intent. If respected, that act signified a willingness to control the self, which was such a significant part of self-government. Violation of the law signified an abandonment of self-control, an unwillingness or inability to balance the common good with personal freedom.

The government represented the consensus of individuals in favor of balancing individual and general welfare. "The whole American government is itself simply a compact with each individual of the thirty millions of persons now inhabitants of These States," Walt Whitman proclaimed, "to protect each one's life, liberty, industry, acquisitions, without excepting one single individual out of the whole number." As Andrew Johnson expressed it, "the soul of liberty was the love of law." Only by what the contemporary historian John

Lothrop Motley called "the constitutional union of the whole people" could violent political discord, anarchy, despotism, and civil war be averted, and individual freedom be safeguarded. The Constitution, as "the basis of all our laws," was the linchpin of free government.[15]

Johnson's phrase "the love of law" referred to a virtue, an acceptance of regulations on individual and collective acts that may upset the balance between personal and common welfare. Self-control, on both the individual and collective levels, was essentially an acceptance of law and of the system of government that embodied and enforced law. Government and law were vital ordering devices for republican society. They prevented self-indulgence from harming the country, allowed the citizen to exploit opportunities presented by the environment, and protected property, livelihoods, and physical existence. Maintaining compliance to the government and its laws was necessary for the maintenance of freedom.[16]

Northerners readily saw a connection between their personal welfare and the governmental-legal system. David Beem, an Indiana soldier, assured his wife that a "good government is the best thing on earth. Property is nothing without it, because it is not protected; a family is nothing without it, because they cannot be educated." People automatically connected concepts such as "the most prosperous nation that ever existed" with the "best govt [sic] ever known."[17]

Thus, the firing on Sumter made sense when Northerners viewed it in this context. Not content to control the South or to form an independent nation of slave states, the slaveholding conspiracy even intended to destroy free institutions in the North. The selfishness, ambition, and belief in brute force that characterized Southerners in Northern minds had outgrown territorial limits; the unprovoked attack on Sumter was proof of the aggressive nature of Southern oligarchy. No longer was the antirepublican South simply an American anachronism; it was now an active, direct, and easily perceived threat to Northern institutions.

The attack on Sumter connoted much more than a bombardment of an isolated army post; it was proof positive that Southerners had gone mad with self-power, had unlearned the art of self-government, and could not be trusted to maintain control of their passions. Most importantly, Sumter proved that this lack of self-control was a direct danger to the South's neighbors. It also proved to Northerners that the values rejected by the South were still vitally important. If allowed to run amuck in North America, the slave power would destroy freedom wherever it expanded. The inevitable surge of unnaturally accumulated power into the domain of liberty—as predicted by republicans of the eighteenth century—had here a clear and simple illustration.

Of the points Northerners could agree on concerning the attack on Sumter, this last one was the strongest. "A deliberate attempt is made to destroy the first popular government that ever existed," wrote Anna Ferris of Wilmington, Delaware, a few days after Sumter fell. Kansas farmer Samuel James Reader had been willing to let the South secede peacefully as late as March 1861. After Sumter he wrote: "It now appears that they want to inaugurate the 'irrepressible conflict' in their own way by taking or destroying the National Capital and then carrying their arms north and subduing all before them." Two years later Northerners continued to comment on the meaning of Sumter in the same way. The federal government was the aggrieved party, waging "a struggle for existence," as an Illinois soldier phrased it. Jane Gray Swisshelm of Minnesota called the firing on Sumter "an open warfare on the fundamental principles of Republican Institutions." All this lent a flavor of desperate defense to the war. "The issue resolves itself into this," reasoned John Stahl Peterson. "The resistance of invasion; the vindication of our manliness as a people; the protection of our own firesides—else be overrun, outraged, desolated, enslaved by the minions of a Southern oligarchy, which indulges the insane conceit that it is born to rule." [18]

The Southern act of violence represented a disregard for law and order. To accept Sumter and the rebellion meant for George Templeton Strong of New York "admitting the principle that there is no social compact binding on any body of men too numerous to be arrested by a United States marshal." The descent into self-aggrandizement epitomized by Sumter represented a descent from national greatness to the status of "merely a great mob." Charles Eliot Norton read Northern reaction to Sumter very clearly. [19]

It was not that their passions were aroused, or that they were seized with the sudden contagion of a short-lived popular excitement,—but all their self-respect, their intelligent and conservative love of order, government, and law, all their instinctive love of liberty, and their sense of responsibility for the safety of the blessings of freedom and of popular government, were stirred to their very depth.

The attack on Sumter, "this invasion of the public order," signified to Northerners an attack on free government. "There is left no choice but between a support of the Government and anarchy!" wrote the editor of the *Boston Post*. Lydia Maria Child was exasperated with English journalists for arguing that the North had no cause to fight for. "Good Heavens! when we are fighting to have *any* government preserved to us! to be saved from utter anarchy!" More specifically, Northern stakes in the contest were, as a Cincinnati editor put it, "constitutional law and the faith of compacts, against anarchy and repudiation."[20]

Northerners saw in the conflict a basic question: whether free government was strong enough to protect itself. Abraham Lincoln set the tone for many who dwelled on this problem when he made his first important speech before Congress after Sumter fell. Dividing power between the government and the governed had insured that both held the necessary power to act. "It is now for them to demonstrate to the world, that those who can fairly carry an election, can also suppress a rebellion—that ballots are the rightful, and peaceful, successors of bullets; and that when ballots have fairly, and constitutionally, decided, there can be no successful appeal, back to bullets."[21]

The attack on Sumter also helped to crystallize in Northern minds the direct opposition between freedom and slavery in the sectional struggle. Of course, many Americans of the antebellum period (including abolitionists and radical Republicans) had already fixed this dichotomy in their minds before 1861. But with Sumter and the general view that the South was an aggressive power aimed directly at Northern institutions, it became a popular notion. Thus, men who had not been enlisted in abolitionist ranks joined old believers in viewing the two sections not only as different in character but as antagonistic as well. Lemuel Adams, a lowly Illinois lieutenant, recalled that he and his friends "were not political abolitionists when we enlisted in the war for the Union . . . but it soon became apparent even to those who had not given much or special thought to the subject that the right to hold

slaves and to take them into any State or territory was the main thing
that the leaders of the rebellion were waging for." Lydia Maria Child,
who had long been concerned about the political evils of the slave
system, proclaimed the conflict[22]

a war to decide whether this is to be a free country, where working-men elect
their own rulers, and where free schools give all an equal chance for education,
or whether we are to live under despotic institutions, which will divide society
into two classes, rulers and servants, and ordain ignorance as the convenient,
nay, even *necessary* condition of all who labor. These are Southern ideas; and
unless the rebels are conquered, they will assuredly invade *us*, and force their
institutions upon the whole country.

Northerners had widespread faith that, at heart, their motivation for
supporting the war was intellectual in nature. People from many walks
of life not only recognized ideas as important but were pleased with
the contrast this made with Southern motives. While their opponents
seemed to be spurred only by selfish impulses, they were convinced
their cause required an intelligent people as its champion.

"*We commenced this war for an idea!*" wrote William Camm, English-
born colonel of the 14th Illinois Infantry. It was "the primal idea on
which America had been founded, according to an army recruiter at
Jeffersonville, Indiana. Both wrote of the ideal of liberty, wrapped up
in American nationalism. Its power to move Northerners was never
better expressed than by a young, articulate Illinois officer in 1863.
Writing to his wife, James Connolly remarked: "Those of us who
looked to the future with high hopes, staked life, reputation, honor,
everything in this contest—taking our lives in our hands we went out
for what? for money? no; for power? no; for fame? no; only for an
idea, for the idea of Union, Freedom, an intangible something always
sought for by mankind, often fought for and never appreciated when
possessed."[23]

Having connected the existence of the American government with
the hope of self-government, Northerners saw an attack on one as an
attack on the other. All of this led to a renewal of patriotic feeling. A
month after the attack on Sumter, Jane Stuart Woolsey of a well-to-do
New York family marveled at the way the attack had energized the
patriotic spirit of the North. "It seems as if we never were alive till

now," she wrote, "never had a country till now. How could we ever have laughed at Fourth-of-Julys?" In its resolve to resist Southern aggression, the government and the people who supported it proved the resiliency of free institutions. Preserving the nation was necessary for the preservation of freedom. "So, 'Republicanism will wash'—*is* washed already in the water and the fire of this fresh baptism," continued Woolsey, "and has a new name, which is *Patriotism*."[24]

The idea of freedom that played such a large role in motivating Northerners represented a curious dilemma. How could Northerners believe in it despite the existence of slavery, the most unfree institution of all? In order to make any sense of this, they had to develop a sectional vision of freedom. It is difficult to tell at what point this crystallized on the popular level; it probably did not fully come to pass until Sumter, although the notion had been slowly building for a long time before.

A certain sense of complacency about their institutions had come to characterize antebellum Northerners.[25] The coexistence of liberty and slavery within the same nation bothered many, but on a popular level it was essential not to dwell on the implications of this dichotomy if one wanted to feel good about oneself and the country. In his memoirs, which reflected the attitudes of most soldiers, Ulysses Grant admitted that before the war he had not been bothered by the issue of whether or not America could remain half-slave and half-free. Politician Henry Winter Davis of Maryland expressed it well when he noted that as long as slavery remained an "interest," on the same political level as the tariff and the currency issue, it could not only be tolerated but prevented from having a harmful influence on free institutions. When slavery became a "power," it upset the peaceful workings of the system and called for extraordinary measures. It was true, as the soldier Albion Tourgee believed, that antebellum Northerners carried within themselves a latent sense that the country was only nominally one nation. In reality, the country consisted of two cultures sharing a common nationality. Freedom and slavery were the distinctive features of those cultures. Indeed, the only restriction on individual liberty in the North was a reluctance to criticize Southerners for fear of antagonizing them and causing dismemberment.[26]

With Sumter, it became easier than ever to see that the slave power wanted to expand beyond its borders. As a result, voices critical of antebellum Northern attitudes were raised. Many now believed that compromise with the South had been motivated by greed for economic prosperity rather than a true desire to preserve peace. It took an aggressive act such as Sumter to awaken the North to the threat posed by slavery. As John Lothrop Motley realized, the war became an effort "to crush forever the doctrine that slavery is the national, common law of America, instead of being an exceptional, local institution confined within express limits."[27]

This was no surprise to certain Northern groups, including radical Republicans and abolitionists. The latter, in their effort to enlighten the upper section regarding the danger of slave power, displayed a national vision of freedom. They tried to rouse the North to a degree of watchfulness similar to the vigilant, ever-active people eighteenth-century republicans had insisted were the best safeguard of liberty. Abolitionists argued that the founding generation had left much undone. In their effort to complete that work, they tried to rouse the North to a national consciousness of freedom and to inspire them to spread liberty to all parts of the nation. They looked to the republican past not to feel self-satisfied but to learn and to capture the energizing spirit of freedom.[28] Viewed as agitators whose work threatened what was to most Northerners a very comfortable status quo, abolitionists did not see their message take effect until Southerners themselves began to prove its validity. It would take some time, however, for the message to sink in.

For most Northerners, the attack on Sumter held connotations of white rather than black slavery. They could live with black bondage and the knowledge that it destroyed white freedom in the South by stifling a middle class and leading to the despotism of slave owners. But they could not live with an attack on free Northern institutions. A Pennsylvania soldier was convinced that fighting for mere political unity would not be understood by the world. It was a rather selfish end with no implications for the wider progress of mankind. But coupling that political unity with "the magic word *Freedom*" would make the war effort sensible to outsiders, by tapping into the rhetoric of liberty many Europeans shared with Americans. Fighting for white political liberty was something everyone could understand.[29] For the first half of the war, Northerners in general gave little consideration to the concept of black freedom.

Of course, abolitionists did not ignore white political liberty in their zeal to destroy slavery, but they focused more sharply on black freedom than did anyone else in America. Chauncey Cooke, a soldier from Wisconsin, proudly displayed his sentiments. "I tell the boys right to their face I am in the war for the freedom of the slave. When they talk about the saving of the Union I tell them that is Dutch to me. I am for helping the slaves if the Union goes to smash." A New Yorker, Walter Stone Poor, believed the Civil War was a nobler contest than the Revolution, for his ancestors had "fought for their own freedom, while we fight for that of another race." Civilians also recognized the inspirational power of an abolitionist war. In April 1861, Swiss immigrant Theodore Bost criticized Northerners for only seeing in the conflict an answer to the question: " 'whether our government is good for something,' that is, whether we can defeat the slave states." A people as unmilitaristic as Americans were needed some higher ideal, such as emancipation, "that would give us real dedication instead of mere excitement."[30]

Abolitionists who recognized that the founding fathers had erred saw their handiwork as flawed. Born in Virginia, but embracing abolition when he moved North, Moncure Conway did not see the Constitution as a gift from Mount Sinai. He saw it as a document that the "fathers themselves acknowledged as necessarily partial, and in many regards temporizing." Unlike most Northerners he did not look on the Constitution as an absolute law. People like Conway had the insight to realize that any legal institution that protected a moral evil was itself morally wrong. Lydia Maria Child pondered this paradox. "Law is not law, if it violates principles of eternal justice." The mass of citizens, blinded by their devotion to law as a safeguard of free government, seemed to have forgotten that statutes could be made by bad men for evil purposes. Because Northerners placed laws on the same exalted level as *fixed principles*," the distinction between moralism and policy became blurred. This moral confusion allowed slavery to exist side by side with liberty. Contrary to most republicans, Child and others like her questioned the virtue, "the state of moral healthfulness," of the Northern people for not modifying the laws to avert this tragedy.[31]

It may well be, as Moncure Conway insisted in 1861, that the Northern decision to wage war after Sumter, instead of compromise, was an implied rejection of the antebellum Union, although very few Northerners would have then seen it that way. In his view, Unionists were the real revolutionaries for they sought to depose the rule of slavery over the United States.[32]

Conway illustrated the more strident picture of liberty that set the abolitionists apart from their countrymen. Abolitionists adhered to a vision that stretched across sectional boundaries and reached back in time to an earlier—to them, more vital—spirit of liberty. Their conception of freedom was in sharp contrast with the popular conception, for it sought to extend opportunity to a race that had traditionally been excluded. The rest of the North, at least those who continued to be wholehearted supporters of the war effort, would not catch up with the abolitionists until the war had progressed a year or more.

Abolitionists were a significant part of Northern prowar support, but they did not represent mainstream opinion. Northerners in and out of uniform fully recognized that the nation's crisis was connected with their identity of America. What gave spirit to their war effort, a spirit absolutely necessary if they were to endure the long, costly war that followed, was the firm belief that they were fighting for vitally important elements of their everyday lives, as well as for an idea that had stimulated people for centuries. Firmly convinced that theirs was the best hope for realizing the long quest for liberty, Northerners felt added responsibility for defending their institutions. They were not only fighting for their own freedom; they were also serving as an example to oppressed people around the world of what could be accomplished with the right combination of intelligence, resources, and faith. It was a weighty combination of self-interest and altruism that was to play a large role in sustaining a bloody war.

CHAPTER 3

Coming to Terms

When they evaluated the relationship between motives and cost, Northerners found a great source of strength in their ideology. It gave them goals that justified the enormous suffering, offered explanations for why the cost was so great, sustained them through periods of doubt on and off the battlefield, and anchored their acceptance of death in righteous, eternal principles. The patriotism of the Civil War generations was strongly grounded and delineated by their values.

Northerners were fascinated with battlefield death and believed it epitomized the real cost of their war effort. Although two soldiers died of illness for every one killed in combat, the public concentrated on battle death as the ultimate tragedy of war. Economic losses were one thing, as Philadelphian Sidney George Fisher put it in May 1861, but the worst was yet to come. "There has been no fighting. When blood has been shed the terrible nature of the conflict will be felt."[1]

Soldiers and civilians recognized that the experience of battle could upset ideological motives. By working on the emotions, it threatened to drive out reasoned estimates of what the war could accomplish for the nation and with that destroy a willingness to accept whatever suffering was needed to accomplish those aims. "It almost takes away all my patriotism to see them," remarked a clergyman of the wounded in Virginia. Cornelia Hancock, a young New Jersey woman who volunteered for field-hospital work at Gettysburg, was stunned by the horrible sights. "I have lost all interest in political affairs," she admitted in letters home, and had "no eyes, ears, for anything but the sufferings of the soldiery." The atmosphere of death at Gettysburg "robbed the battlefield of its glory, the survivors of their victory, and the wounded of what little chance of life was left to them."[2]

No one more appropriately phrased the effect battle could have on the thinking process and on the role of ideas as motives than Abner Small of Maine. A soldier who saw the worst of the 1864–65 fighting in Virginia, he wrote one of the most moving memoirs to come from the war. "The bravest front, bolstered by pride and heroic resolution, will crumble in the presence of the agony of wounds," Small reported. "Wading through bloody fields and among the distorted dead bodies of comrades, dodging shells, and posing as a target to hissing bullets that whisper of eternity, is not conducive to continuity of action, much less of thought. The shock from a bursting shell will scatter a man's thoughts as the iron fragments will scatter the leaves overhead." In Small's hardened opinion, the battlefield was no place for an ideologue.[3]

When Northerners asserted ideology as the motive and aim of their war, they made a conscious effort to defy the experience of battle and all it implied about subordinating ideas to emotions and physical safety. By sustaining the war effort, they continued to hold the idea of liberty as a viable model of government. They believed that support for the Northern form of governance was support for freedom.

"Better lose a million men in battle than allow the government to be overthrown," wrote army officer and future president James Garfield. Adin Ballou, an obscure private in the 10th Maine Infantry, echoed Garfield's sentiments. Ruminating on battle and "suspicious [sic] that Death is creeping behind me with his fatal dart," Ballou assured his wife that he knew "how American Civilization now leans upon the triumph of the Government and how great a debt we owe to those who went before us through the blood and suffering of the Revolution; and I am willing perfectly willing to lay down all my joys in this life to help maintain this Government."[4]

Although much of this rhetoric appeared before the soldier experienced battle, it continued even after he fought and suffered. Before his first engagement, Dietrich Smith of Illinois had often written of his willingness to die for the cause. Suffering a shoulder wound at Shiloh, he did not lose his enthusiasm for the values he believed his nation embodied. Even as the wound continued to discharge bone fragments, he repeated his willingness to return to duty.[5]

The inevitable suffering severely tested motives, and many Northerners were able to affirm their convictions only after wracking doubts. The experience of war had the power to turn an individual in on himself, and to drive his thoughts inward and away from contemplation of the larger good. The suffering had the power to make Northerners self-centered and obsessed with their emotional and physical pain, forgetting the goals that could benefit the nation as well as themselves.

Ebenezer Hannaford of Ohio left an amazing description of his wound and near death at Stone's River. He was unique only in his ability to write engrossingly about it, for his experience represented that of thousands of his less-articulate comrades. Severely wounded in the neck, Hannaford found his thoughts absorbed by the physical effects of the wound. Nothing seemed to concern him but the pain. Not until he found a relatively quiet, safe place to hide from the bullets, where he believed he would die, did he have an opportunity to ponder the meaning of his sacrifice. "Thank God, death did not seem so dreadful," he reasoned, "now that it was come. And then the sacrifice was not all in vain, falling thus in God's own holy cause of Freedom."[6]

Sent to a Nashville hospital, Hannaford faced many months of uncertain recovery. It was a horrible time during which he became obsessed with the thought of dying. On two occasions Hannaford's neck wound hemorrhaged, and he nearly lost his life. The end result of this slow agony became palpable to him in the hospital rooms. "It was there that Death drew near and bent over my pillow, so close that I could feel his icy breath upon my cheek, while in mute, ghastly silence we looked steadfastly each in the other's face for weeks together." Indeed, Hannaford felt such peaceful release ("a quiet, painless lethargy was stealing over my brain") that on one occasion when his wound bled profusely, splattering the nearby wall with red patches, he felt angry at the doctor for stopping the flow of blood and bringing him back to consciousness. "Those moments of syncope, when over my soul had rolled the waters of oblivion, I seemed to feel had been a very heaven of delight, and it was pitiful service to recall me thence to life and suffering again."[7]

Hannaford spent over a year in hospitals before his neck had healed enough that he was able to return home. For months on end, his wound drew his thoughts away form the war and into himself. It was not until his fellow patients, engaged in a songfest to pass away the time, happened to sing "The Battle Cry of Freedom" that his consciousness recalled the larger meanings of the war. No other song of the North better expressed the basic motive for fighting. For Hannaford, its sentiments justified the long months of agony. The song "thrilled me inexpressibly," he recalled later. "The early days of the war; the grand uprising of the loyal North; the wild burning enthusiasm of those Sumter times . . . the grand infinitude of principle—of Right, and Truth, and Justice—that was underlying the whole fierce struggle, and had made our Cause one that it was, oh! how noble a thing to have fought and suffered for, and, if need be, yet to die for!"[8]

Civilians no less than combatants had to face the doubts induced by battle and its aftermath. Most Northern families had loved-ones in the armies, and even those who personally knew no soldiers were faced with the fact that large-scale casualties were a national loss, as well as the aggregate of many individual losses. The emotional journeys of three civilians spoke for thousands more who left no record of their struggle with the question of motive and cost.

Ruth A. Whittemore was twenty-four years old and living in Owego, New York, when the war began. Her brother Charles drove an ambulance in the 50th New York Engineers, and to him Ruth wrote of her faith in the war and its aims. The conflict involved questions of "right over wrong, of Justice over Injustice and Rebellion"; it was a fight against the "despotism of traitors" that justified all sacrifices. In June 1862, the possibility that Charles may have to join the firing lines dampened her enthusiasm. She tried to persuade him to remain with the ambulances. "I think you are doing your duty just as much and are entitled to just as much honor and render your country as good a service as those that shoot down and fight the rebels. Your life is imperiled the same as theirs."[9]

The threat of personal loss began to curb Whittemore's strident patriotism. With the bloody battles of 1862, she also began to feel the general impact of her support for the war. "Oh! it is an awful thing for so many men to go there to be mowed down like the grass and their precious lives and blood poured out like water on the burning soil of those inhuman bloodhounds," she moaned. "I think of it all the time lately and fear that we do not know the end." For Whittemore, the loss of Northern manhood represented her personal stake in the army writ large. "It seems as though the war is coming nearer home every day," she wrote Charles in December 1862. "When we think of the brothers that have gone and that they are liable to be called into battle at any minute I tell you it comes pretty close to our hearts." The suspense after Chancellorsville was almost too much to bear. When a letter finally arrived from Charles, Whittemore cried for joy. "I had felt so bad before that it seemed as though I should choke. O! when will this wicked war end and the precious blood cease to flow? The stain must forever blot this nation's history." She told Charles how news of the death or injury of an acquaintance could bring home the cost of the war. "We ought to remember that for every one that falls on the battlefield or suffers a languishing death in the hospitals, some friends mourn and weep their lives away."[10]

Yet Ruth Whittemore came to accept the emotional suffering. She endured a sequence of fervent enthusiasm, later apprehension, and final acceptance. After her exposure to the sanguinary nature of combat in 1862, she reaffirmed her commitment to the war. "I have no doubts and have never had as to the final result," she believed in mid-1863, "but I sometimes get impatient to see it brought about."[11]

Anna Ferris, a forty-six-year-old resident of Wilmington, Delaware, had no illusions about suffering in war. She was disturbed by the festive Christmas celebration of 1861, believing the nation would have to suffer sooner or later and might as well learn to deal with it. "We cannot expect victory to be so cheaply bought," she confided to her diary, and "if we are not to achieve victory, we must surely wear our sackcloth and ashes." Ferris was convinced that "the permanence of our Government is to be worth all it can possibly cost," yet she had no patience with those who ignored the price. A sensitive woman, she could not forget "the horrors that lie beneath" military victory. Ferris agonized while awaiting battle news, wondering how someone with a loved-one in the army endured while she, with no soldier acquaintance, could hardly bear the suspense.[12]

Ferris represented a healthy attitude toward the balance sheet between motive and cost. A firm believer in the former, she refused to lose sight of the latter. Therefore, she never lost touch with the human drama of the war. It strengthened the worth of Union victory to remember the suffering endured for it. "Through a Red Sea of blood," she wrote in April 1865, "through a long struggle of suffering & agony, the promised land of peace & liberty is reached at last & the end now that it is attained, seems worth the struggle, dreadful as it has been."[13]

Like Ferris, the poet Walt Whitman never let himself forget that war resulted in human suffering. Until the battle of Fredericksburg, he remained in the North writing affirmative poetry about the political aspects of the conflict. Traveling to Washington to nurse a wounded brother, Whitman became obsessed with the injured. Thus began his inner battle regarding motive and cost.

After working for a few months in the hospitals, Whitman admitted that "to see what I see so much of, puts one entirely out of conceit of war—still for all that I am not sure but I go in for fighting on—the choice is hard on either part, but to *cave* in the worst." Trying to imagine the casualties at Gettysburg, he confessed to his mother that "every once in a while I feel so horrified & disgusted—it seems to me like a great slaughter-house & the men mutually butchering each other—then I feel how impossible it appears, again, to retire from this contest, until we have carried our points—(it is cruel to be so tossed from pillar to post in one's judgment)." Whitman continually paired affirmation of the war's goals with recognition of their horrible cost. Writing to a soldier friend, he proclaimed it as destined that the Union should win: "It may be long, or it may be short, but that will be the result—but O what precious lives have been lost by tens of thousands in the struggle already."[14]

Like Ruth Whittemore, Whitman was troubled by the threat of personal loss as well as by the oppressive fact of national loss. His brother constantly faced danger in the army. "I get thinking about it sometimes, & it works upon me so I have to stop & turn my mind on something else." Long months in the hospitals and the prospect of even more bloody work in the spring campaigns of 1864 nearly brought

Whitman to an emotional breakdown. Preparations for large numbers of wounded in the Washington hospitals made him remember injured soldiers with whom he had previously worked. "I can hardly believe my own recollections—what an awful thing war is." He believed attendants grew more callous toward the sufferers, their quantity leading to indifference among those charged with their care. "I get almost frightened at the world—Mother, I will try to write more cheerfully next time—but I see so much."[15]

Whitman was saved from sinking too deeply into morose thoughts by influences outside the hospitals. For example, it took little more than news of antiwar dissent within Congress to shore up his support for the conflict. To the extent that he could allow outside events to intrude on his self-contained world inside the hospitals, Whitman could hope to avoid the threat to his reasoned acceptance of the war. It allowed him to regain contact with the enthusiasm for the war he had felt before entering the hospitals, although his support was now tempered by greater knowledge. He admitted that after Fredericksburg he had doubts not about the worth of the war but about the ability of Northern leaders to carry it through: "but that has past [sic] away, the war *must* be carried on." He even expressed a willingness to enter the ranks himself—although not suited for the life of a soldier—if he could better aid the cause in that way. By late May 1864, with the bloody fighting in Virginia and Georgia at its peak, Whitman was secure enough in his attitude toward the conflict to believe that losing a loved-one in battle "would be tempered with much to take the edge off. . . . It would be a noble & manly death, & in the best cause." He believed that death held fewer terrors for the soldier who lay dying in a hospital than the public imagined.[16]

Whitman spoke not in ignorance but from many months of devoted, almost daily work with the sick and wounded. He achieved his support for the war after an emotional roller-coaster ride. One of the most sensitive civilians to encounter battle suffering, he never let himself forget the human drama of war; indeed, he pursued it with a poet's intensity. His *Drum-Taps*, published in early 1865, hinted at this drama. Whitman waited, however, until a decade had passed before fully exploring in *Memoranda During the War* what he had learned and experienced about men in battle. While the conflict remained undecided, there was little time for anything but maintaining the struggle, and *Drum-Taps* was intended as a tool in that process.

Whittemore, Ferris, and Whitman were the kind of Northerners Ralph Waldo Emerson had in mind when, in the first of his lecture series on American Life delivered in November 1864, he spoke of the people's considered resolve to continue the war. "What gives the greatest weight to this decision is, that it has been made by a people sobered by the calamities of the war, the sacrifice of life, the waste of property, the burden of taxes, and the uncertainties of the result." Without the informed consent of thinking people, such a costly war effort could not have been sustained. The citizen had to understand the value of the war's goals and be aware of their cost. Many Northerners could maintian their support for the war despite—or because of—their ignorance of its emotional cost, but those who learned its bloody lesson and still retained faith in the goals were the solid core of the war effort.[17]

These men and women realized the full weight of the nation's loss. It was a new lesson for America, learning to accept "this tragic and tender lore" of "maimed, ghastly, dying, dead." The wife of William Henry Furness, a Unitarian clergyman in Philadelphia, wrote in the *Atlantic Monthly:* "We knew that we, whom God had hitherto so blessed that we were compelled to look into the annals of other nations for misery and strife, had now commenced a record of our own."[18]

By the thousands, Northern soldiers and civilians came to a personal understanding of life sacrificed for liberty. Nineteen-year-old Montgomery Woodruff was a civilian clerk working for the army in St. Louis. He copied the order to fire a salute in honor of the victory at Fort Donelson, and in his boyish enthusiasm felt as if he had had a hand in the victory itself. His illusions were shattered a few weeks later when the wounded came streaming into the city from Shiloh. "This picture upon which I looked at the St. Louis levee," he ruminated, "was a picture of the price which it costs to have victory, the 'one country and the one flag,' and every man looking upon it stood awed to silence while he looked." Rather than destroying his patriotism, the experience caused Woodruff to more maturely assess the implications of supporting the war. It was a mature judgment because the jingoistic, adventuresome tone of his patriotism had been eliminated by the sight of wounded on the levee, leaving him with a sober statement of the nation's needs. Woodruff concluded that "in the country's time of peril, a soldier's life was a good life, and a soldier's death was a good death." He then joined the army and served well.[19]

Estelle Morrow of Lebanon, Indiana, was a civilian who experienced much the same process of nervousness, shock, and resolution that mirrored the soldier's initiation into battle. In January 1862, keyed up by consistent newspaper reports of impending combat, she hoped the fighting would begin if for no other reason than to end her anxiety about the future. Morrow was heartstruck when news of Shiloh's fearful result arrived. "Oh! how dreadful it is," she wrote in her diary. "I felt sick all the evening after hearing the news, could scarcely refrain from crying. Woke up with a headache this morning. How many poor hearts are weighed down with sorrow, a mourning nation have we this morning. Although we were victorious we cannot think of it." But loss led to a kind of grimness. Morrow accepted the fact of battlefield death writ large, and this acceptance undercut any tendency to forget the issues involved in the war. Six weeks after Shiloh Morrow judged: "Still we are becoming [sic] hardened to the war, as it were, for now with much more calmness we can hear of battles than at first."[20]

Soldiers passed on their knowledge of the war's costs to the people at home. Henry Henney of Ohio warned that "a super-abundance of patriotism" was necessary for anyone contemplating a soldier's life. He was convinced that suffering may "sear our perspective of the love of country" but could not destroy it. "I am inclined to think that the tough experiences have but served to endear our institutions more firmly in our minds." Henney's opinion was supported by other combatants who arrived at a firm resolution to continue the war despite the unexpectedly high casualties. Daniel Holt, the surgeon of the 121st New York Infantry, was shocked but not destroyed by the carnage of Chancellorsville. "I hope never again to be in such a fight; yet today, if necessary, I am willing to follow our noble boys and share their fate, in the effort to redeem our common country." Rather than "recede an inch from God-inspired principle of freedom," Holt was determined to "see the same scenes of bloodshed re-enacted everyday, until a perpetual and honorable peace is secured."[21]

Exposed to the sight of casualties on the field, combatants often paired affirmation of the war with mention of these heart-sickening sights. A militiaman who gazed upon blackened and bloated corpses at Antietam, an experience shocking "enough to overthrow all imaginations concerning the glory of war," retained his faith. "I hope and believe that I would be willing to suffer the worst, to die, if necessary, and leave my body to blacken on the field, rather than prove a traitor to the trust which our country reposes in all her sons."[22]

This militiaman knew that coming to terms with the war's costs was necessary if the goals believed worthy of a great nation were to be gained. Yet that did not mean combatants had to lose all sentiment. John Russell, an Illinois infantryman and one of the strongest supporters of the war, reacted to Shiloh by writing home: "Our hearts have just been made glad over the great victory at Pittsburg [Landing], but sorrowful at the frightful loss of life that it cost, to win it." The abolitionist and New York artilleryman William Wheeler saw the badly dug graves of his own men on the field of Second Bull Run. "I was very much depressed by the whole sight, but not shaken in my old resolution to see the end of the matter, or be like these poor men."[23]

For those who provided the main strength of the Union war effort, armed conflict had long ceased to be a glorious march into the history books. Knowledge of the suffering endured by both combatants and mourning civilians came to coexist with ideological motives matured by experience. A visiting English journalist saw this represented in a New York City park where two hastily constructed sheds stood side by side. One was a recruiting station and the other received wounded from McClellan's disastrous Peninsular campaign. Next to the recruiting sergeant stood the torn remnants of once healthy men. The Englishman saw in this juxtaposition something of the Northern people's strength. "There was an air of resolution and stern purpose, given by the contrast of the wounded veteran and the raw recruit, which was not without promise."[24] A people who could reconcile patriotism with the cost of war were well on their way toward sustaining the bloodiest conflict of their history.

Northern support for the war was firmly grounded in the matrix of values current in mid-nineteenth-century America. This was a powerful ordering device for the Northern approach to the problem of motives versus cost, providing guidance for the people's sense of reasonable sacrifice. On the individual and collective levels, Northerners worked out a belief that the losses were not too high for the aims of the war. In one way or another, several cultural features aided them in this belief.

Self-control was an example. One of the most pervasive themes in the soldier's description of battle was his triumph over inner urges that ran counter to the concern for the good of the whole. When the soldier walked into the killing zone, he entered an environment that led to the release of the most fundamental survival instincts, which overwhelmed his commitment to self-sacrifice. The confusion and terror of battle could drive out any conviction of why the war was fought. The chaos broke down thought processes and turned the soldier inward to raw, overpowering feelings of fear. The soldier could lose his self-possession, become "unmanned" (to use a popular nineteenth-century expression), and forsake his duty to the army and to the nation. Control of selfish passions was the hallmark of a good citizen, and supporting the federal government in a war designed to preserve free government was itself an act of citizenship. By emphasizing their self-command in this horrifying environment, combatants asserted their self-image as good Americans.

There were, of course, other reasons for maintaining coolness in battle, for a soldier was only as good as his nerve and determination. "If you go into a fight," advised an Illinois father to his son, "keep *cool* so that you can exercise good judgement, don't shake in your boots, in fact think of nothing, but how you may but do your duty." Iowa General William Belknap believed that self-control, along with devotion to the principles motivating the war effort, were the key qualities of a good soldier. No matter how sound his convictions, a man was no use on the battlefield if he did not have enough self-discipline to load and fire.[25]

But the emphasis on self-control spoke to a deeper meaning as well. Soldiers realized it was a test of their manhood and of their ability to maintain control of passion in order to fulfill civic obligation. Therefore, testing the nerves in battle was also a process of self-exploration. "I now know myself better than I did before," wrote Pennsylvanian Jacob Heffelfinger after his first battle. "I have always been afraid, that notwithstanding my firm resolve to do my duty, I would become so excited in the hour of battle as to lose my presence of mind and perhaps find myself acting the coward without knowing it." Proving the power of self-command was also confirmation that the individual possessed the qualities needed by all good citizens.[26]

No one expressed this more openly than did John Rankin of the 27th Indiana Infantry. He believed that most soldiers had to deal with the conflict of self-interest and the common good at least once in their war careers. As Rankin marched in line at the battle of Antietam his mind became preoccupied with survival. Realizing that his position on the far end of the regimental line did not exempt him from receiving the full weight of enemy fire, he devised a plan to leave the field with honor by helping wounded comrades to the rear. When his captain fell, Rankin jumped quickly to his side but not fast enough to beat another private with the same intention.[27]

Rankin's impulse to save himself at the expense of his larger duty failed. Returning to his place in line, he began to ponder why he had acted so selfishly and to think of what effect on the war effort a victory or defeat at Antietam could have. "Gradually I lose my desire to leave the field," he remarked later. "An intense anxiety as to the result of the struggle comes on. My own possible fate is entirely foreign to my thoughts. A full realization of the awful possibilities involved in the battle fully possesses me." Thinking about the cause and all it embodied was the key to avoiding the threat posed by combat to ideological motives. "Thank God! my higher nature has triumphed," Rankin continued. "It has lifted me out of the mire of self and cowardice in which I floundered. . . . This army may be swept from the field before sunset; within a moment I may be a mangled corpse; I may sleep in an unknown grave; but, come what may, I am a victor over self."[28]

Rankin was not alone in thinking that the struggle between self and the whole was connected with the war and the goals involved in it. Twelve days after having been deeply involved in the horrors of Fredericksburg, Walter Carter of Massachusetts wrote: *"Rely upon me when duty calls, for my sense of right and love of country and its glorious cause would impel me forward to death, even if my poor weak nature hung back and human feelings gained control over me.* . . . I never lose self-control I care not for myself."[29]

The ideal of self-control was only one factor in building support for

the war. In order to maintain the balance between high casualties and
the conflict's goals, Northerners had to have a powerful belief in the
principles they fought for and a regard for life that was not so overwhelming as to kill the acceptance of sacrifice. Throughout the North,
people asserted their allegiance to the principles; the casualties forced
them to evaluate their conceptions of life and death.

Charles Eliot Norton, one of the North's most thoughtful conservative intellectuals, addressed the question with vigor and frankness. He
believed that the defeat at First Bull Run should have been taken as a
lesson of the expendability of life. Norton agreed that American society should nurture a high regard for individualism but thought that
"feeble sentimentalities, and false estimates of its value" had often
resulted. Northerners had to realize that war called for an awareness
of things higher than life and less dreadful than death. "It is not often
that men can have the privilege to offer their lives for a principle; and
when the opportunity comes, it is only the coward that does not
welcome it with gladness. Life is of no value in comparison with the
spiritual principles from which it gains its worth. . . . Self-preserva-
tion must yield to Truth's preservation."[30]

Unitarian minister James Freeman Clarke of Boston came to the
same conclusion. His views were confirmed by a visit to Gettysburg
to find a wounded relative. What he saw there among the injured
impressed him. The soldiers appeared to understand more clearly as
time went by that the war was a contest "between liberty and slavery,
between civilization and barbarism, between Christianity and Anti-
christ." This was the sustaining power behind their willingness to
endure battle injury. Clarke wrote in awe of the "supreme peace of
men who seem to have lost everything that makes life worth having. I
saw men maimed, crippled for life; but they all said, 'No matter, we
beat them.' I saw a man who had lost both his eyes; but he was
cheerful, even merry. One man who had lost a foot said, 'I would
rather have lost the other than not have won the victory.' "[31]

Clarke felt he could not grieve for men who held such sentiments
but that he should rejoice in their spirit. He believed that his was not
yet a degenerate people but was still capable, as was the Revolutionary
generation, of self-sacrifice for a worthy goal. The same capacity for
self-control in the face of personal agony was evident among loved-

ones left behind. "I visit their mothers or sisters, their fathers or brothers," Clarke said in a sermon, "when the fatal news arrives. I go with fear, dreading to meet a great and hopeless anguish. I find heaven there. I find the peace of God in their souls. I go to carry sympathy, and words of comfort; but I receive instead inspiration."[32]

Abolitionist Thomas Wentworth Higginson agreed that the losses were not too great for the goal of emancipation. While a civilian at Worcester, Massachusetts, he asserted that the war had not affected the price of gunpowder, "because the amount used does not exceed the amount ordinarily expended in field sports. And so against the losses in battle we must set the lives saved from home disease and dangers." His wife believed that Higginson thought crossing Worcester's Main Street was more dangerous than exposing oneself in combat, and Higginson admitted there was a grain of truth in it. His point, however, was to show that any effort to achieve a desirable goal involved a certain amount of physical danger. Northerners willingly accepted those dangers in civilian life; why should they shrink from battle when the goals were so much greater?[33]

Other members of the North's intellectual elite found sacrifice for the war's issues a worthy way to end life. Lydia Maria Child consoled the mother of Robert Gould Shaw by reminding her of the "great principles" for which he died. Such a sacrifice was more dear "than a life spent in self-indulgence, gradually impairing the health, and weakening the mental powers." Ralph Waldo Emerson struck the same positive note when writing to the parents of an officer lost at Port Hudson. He predicted that "one whole generation might well consent to perish, if, by their fall, political liberty & clean & just life could be made sure to the generations that follow."[34]

More obscure Northerners echoed Higginson's attempt to show that battle losses were little more than the normal run of civilian death in their emotional impact. Mary Christian Percy described the effects of a fever that ravaged her upstate New York town. "Death stalks through cities & villages quite as mercilessly as upon the battle-field," she reasoned, "only it is here by slow disease that he wills them away, & there, it is the bullet." An Ohio colonel found it difficult to believe that statistically the army lost more men in battle than disease claimed in civilian life. There is no objective evidence to support the claim that the army's death rate equaled that of civilians. Yet, these people made the point that dying was a natural fact of life in or out of the army and that battle sacrifice was only one of many forms of death.[35]

Throughout the North, soldiers and civilians, elites and commoners, the powerful and the obscure joined in the same chorus. The belief that goals exceeded costs pervaded the North. Abraham Lincoln, the common man who became an uncommon president, cogently expressed it in his typically lean, straightforward prose. "We accepted this war for an object," he told an audience at Philadelphia's Sanitary Fair in June 1864. Even as the long casualty lists poured in from Virginia and Georgia, Lincoln counted the Northern goal "a worthy object, and the war will end when that object is attained."[36]

Among members of the lower social ranks, the belief that life was worth giving up for the right cause was encouraged by a pragmatic attitude toward death. Dying took place in the home, and the family was responsible for the preparation and burial of the remains. The "intimacy most people had with death" produced a realistic knowledge of dying as a natural, inevitable part of everyone's life.[37]

Still, a pragmatic acceptance of death by itself could never have led to willing sacrifice on the battlefield. There had to exist a higher, socially approved reason for it. As a result, the prospect of dying in battle often affected men much less than one would expect. Soon after Shiloh, W. H. Clune of the 6th Iowa Infantry dwelled on the meaning of death. "Of how little consequence is the life of any of us. A few tears are shed, the hearth stone for a few days is desolate, then smiles return, mirth and festivity are guests, and in the brief period of a decade, even his family have forgotten him." Illinois soldier Onley Andrus mixed pragmatism and self-sacrifice when he wrote: "If I should [die] it won't kill anybody else but me."[38]

The combination of a pragmatic attitude toward dying and a good cause for which to fight made the horror of battle-death controllable, enabling soldiers and civilians to do what was necessary to prosecute the war. Death, in fact, was viewed as preferable to other war-related threats to nineteenth-century sensibilities. Improper care of the remains was horrifying to many Northerners. "I don't fear to go into battle," admitted Walter Carter of Massachusetts, "neither do I fear wounds, or even death itself . . . but it is the thought that I shall be uncared for, that I shall be buried where no loving hand can strew flowers and shed tears of love over my grave" that upset him. No wonder when, as one soldier reported, burial parties accompanied their digging with "ribald" jokes. William Wheeler pinpointed the disruption of social peace and order by armies, military law, and guerrilla fighting as far worse for the country than was death on the battlefield for individual soldiers.[39]

Because of its emphasis on individualism, Northern culture placed great value on the citizen as an autonomous element of society. Even though individualism held the potential to foster selfishness, it also held the potential for even more giving of self. The citizen had control over how he was to dispose of his talent and of himself. As a free agent, he had the option of joining the army and fighting for a cause his culture taught him to regard as of transcendent importance. He could—and did by the hundreds of thousands—decide that freedom on the personal level was sordid, if not useless, if it was safeguarded at the expense of a system of governance that had insured him the opportunity to decide his own fate.

Thus individualism was a prominent theme in discussion about the value of life, the significance of battle suffering, and the worth of the war effort. Many Northerners reacted differently when confronted with large, impersonal losses than when battle threatened a significant someone close to their hearts. As we have already seen, some men and women took impersonal losses emotionally, for they were sensitive to the nation's suffering as well as to their own. But for many others, the knowledge of large-scale casualties, in the absence of personal connections with the battlefield, was not enough to stir feelings of loss.

Samuel Osgood, a New York minister, noted this insensitivity to the losses in a *Harper's* article. He believed that his contemporaries regarded life in view of universal laws and social statistics and that they considered the war in a similar way: "We find ourselves applying general averages to its issues, and counting the probable percentage of death by battle or disease." This was a distanced, and therefore highly ordered vision of the nation's loss. It tended to impersonalize the cost of achieving war aims. "Tell a woman, for example, that a thousand men were slain in the last battle," Osgood suggested, "and she receives the news with amazement, perhaps with horror, yet does not lose her composure nearly so much as when she hears that one of her own acquaintances was among the number; and as she thinks of him in the agonies of death, she sees the whole thousand who suffered with him, and the *many* appear before her in the *one*." Oliver Wendell Holmes, Sr., understood Osgood's point. While traveling to the Antietam battlefield looking for his son, he saw a group of wounded soldiers and remarked of the "joint-stock of their suffering; it was next to impossible to individualize it, and so bring it home as one can do a single broken limb or aching wound."[40]

It was important to many Northerners that their countrymen feel emotionally involved in the conflict, and individualizing battle suffering was the surest way to achieve this. They believed that a war that had assumed the scope, intensity, and significance of their conflict could be won only if the energy of the North was intensely focused on its prosecution. "People consider the whole matter far too lightly in my opinion," complained Jim Higginson, an upper-crust Bostonian, "in fact they hardly feel the war, excepting through the death of a relative now and then." The commentary of the time was filled with this theme. An acquaintance of Indiana schoolteacher Estelle Morrow grimly told her that "the war is not going to end until we all individually feel that we have much to sacrifice." Soldiers, who had no trouble realizing they could lose everything in the war, were often bitterly happy when Confederates raided Northern territory. They thought it a good lesson for complacent civilians, whom they often suspected of lax support for the war.[41]

In this there was an ironic dilemma. If someone individualized battle suffering, it brought the meaning of the war's cost home; but it also increased the possibility that the horror of the conflict could threaten his motivation. It was one thing to support a war fought by strangers for one's benefit; it was far more difficult to support a war conducted by people you loved. Vermonter Helen Myers poured out her anxiety in a letter to her soldier-brother. "Oh Ed, this war is terrible. It makes me sick to think of it, and while I want the rebellion put down, I cannot bear the thought that my friends must have a hand in it, and especially my brothers. There is not much of the spirit of '76 in me."[42]

This woman's dilemma was a microcosm of the Northern war effort, representing in one case what hundreds of thousands of people had to face. Those who constituted the backbone of the war effort met this dilemma squarely and concluded that even the personal loss of a dear friend or relative had to be endured if the principles involved in the conflict called for it. Myers did this by remaining a supporter of the war and by getting used to the thought of her brother's exposure to death. She did it all in a very frank manner. "Now don't be vexed with me because I have not more patriotism," she coaxed Ed. "I cannot help feeling so, and will not deny it. I would not have you act the coward, but don't be rash and throw yourself into the very face of death unnecessarily." Myers was wrong; she was patriotic. But her patriotism was of the mature, stolid variety. It was quite different from the jingoistic puffing of those who urged soldiers to needlessly expose themselves in order to prove their loyalty to the war effort. She accepted the danger to her brother without losing her faith that the war is worth fighting.[43]

Helen Myers suggested that the balance sheet between motive and cost did not result from a clear-cut triumph of convictions over death. For her, it was a willing yet troubled understanding with the dice-throw of danger. In their acceptance of battle sacrifice, Northerners never forgot the individual and the inherent value of a human life. The journalist John Trowbridge toured battlefields just after the war. He went to Gettysburg in an effort to reconstruct the individual lives of so many thousands of unknown dead. As he gazed upon the graves, he tried to recall that each man "had his interests, his loves, his darling hopes, the same as you or I. All were laid down with his life. It was no trifle to him, it was as great a thing to him as it would be to you." Although the war was over, Trowbridge wanted himself and his readers to reexperience the true weight of the nation's loss by thinking of the dead as individuals: "not insensible to danger, but braving it— these men . . . confronted, for their country's sake, that awful uncertainty. Did they believe in your better world? Whether they did or not, this world was a reality, and dear to them."[44]

Trowbridge did not want the value of the individual to be forgotten in the willingness to sacrifice for the cause. The yearning to maintain individualism in the midst of large-scale carnage and impersonalized war was strong in the North and was illustrated by the concept of the soldier's sacrifice. Northerners believed that the deaths of virtuous men served as good examples for their society—a notion that is common to most cultures. The Russian emigré Nadine Turchin asserted her faith in battle death as leading to something better for the Northern cause. "The moral sense of civilized man accepts quite willingly this kind of sacrifice."[45]

Northerners incorporated this common trait into their faith in the war effort. One of the more eloquent spokesmen for the ideal of regeneration through sacrifice was Jane Grey Swisshelm, a nurse in Washington who wrote dispatches for a Minnesota newspaper. She described a fallen soldier in language that left no doubt in her reader's mind as to his worthiness. "With his highly cultivated intelligence and keen appreciation of the good and true he could not do otherwise than fight for principle—the principle of self-government." After identifying his virtue with the goals of the war, Swisshelm applauded the connection as predestined for glory. God chose the soldier to die in this war, and it was a "sublime mission" for such a worthy individual. It was useless for the survivors to weep, according to Swisshelm, for "in reality it is we who shall die 'Like a dull worm to rot/ Cast foully in the earth to be forgot' who should weep for ourselves and one another. Those who have died for a great purpose and gone directly to their great reward are the favored few."[46]

It was easier to accept the loss of men if the soldiers were seen as exemplars of all that was good in Americans; thus reinforcing self-images of the nation, the culture, and the issues involved in the war. An Illinois soldier named Howard Stevens was less eloquent but just as committed to the ideal as was Swisshelm. Writing of his brother who was killed during the Vicksburg campaign, he pondered the meaning of a death that struck close to his heart: "The blood of our fallen heroes will purify and place an indellible [sic] stamp of true patriotism upon this cursed [sic] soil and every hero that falls will be as a nail driven in a sure place rendering the Union one and inseperable [sic] forever hereafter." A civilian named Ebey traveled to Shiloh, where he had lost a son and a brother-in-law and where another son had been wounded. William Camm, the commander of this man's relatives, recalled Ebey's words at a dinner held just before the regiment left Illinois. "Colonel, I will give my last son, my last dollar, and my own life to put down this rebellion." Ebey's loss at Shiloh did not change his conviction. Visiting the spot where his son had been killed, where dark red still stained the earth, Ebey took "a wild ground willow pulled out of the blood of his son to carry home to plant." In his quietly poetic way, Ebey demonstrated the regenerative value of his son's sacrifice.[47]

Adherence to the ideal of sacrifice assumed such virile proportions that soldiers often expressed a preference for injury or death—if that were their fate—to occur in some combat-related act rather than by disease or accident. "I tell you there is no *honor* in a man's *sickness*," complained Stephen Rogers of Massachusetts as he lay ill in a hospital in the East, "but there is about a *wound* in the minds of most men." This curious yearning to be maimed by the enemy rather than by a sordid agent was summed up in the anguished cry of an Ohio soldier accidently shot in the foot by a comrade. "Oh, if it had only been a secession ball I wouldn't have cared." Accidental death, a common occurrence in the army, seemed to cancel all that was worthy about dying for one's country. After losing many comrades while crossing the White River of Arkansas, Benjamin McIntyre, a soldier of the 19th Iowa Infantry, pondered the meaning of a soldier's death. He had witnessed many men die in battle and of wounds but had been encouraged to continue to fight because of what he had seen. "Yet in their death there was something sublime and they seemed to feel that to die in such a cause was heroic and left its lesson upon our memory that we were left to avenge their death." But to drown on a rickety ferry and "to sacrafice [sic] all for the sake of their country and then to find such a grave" was somehow sordid and dispiriting.[48]

As a perceptive newspaper correspondent pointed out, there was an air of fantasy in all the rhetoric about regeneration through the soldier's sacrifice. This reporter doubted whether anyone truly felt happiness at giving up his life for his country. Yet, this "absurd invention" filled letters of consolation written by comrades to loved ones of the deceased. The reporter missed the point. It was not the question of truth but aspiration that was important. To assert this deathbed sentiment was an effort to balance motive and cost, to shore up the war effort, and to reaffirm the value of the individual. The soldier was not a beef led to slaughter, as Ernest Hemingway would later put it, but a free-agent who willingly gave his most precious possession for a cause that gained further value with each freely given, virtuous life sacrificed for it.[49]

It mattered little to Edward Payson Goodwin, a Christian Commission worker in the Washington hospitals, that the dying lieutenant he observed was delirious and therefore not capable of uttering reasoned, willing sentiments of sacrifice. When the soldier shouted, "F-o-r-w-a-r-d! Double quick! March!!" the worker understood the soldier's rallying cry to be a spectacular affirmation of devotion to the cause—even on the threshold of eternity. "Ah! What a sublime heroism these noble boys do carry in their bosoms," Goodwin exulted. Less naive, and therefore speaking more directly to the heart of the war experience, was the response of parents whose son had been lost in the Seven Days fighting. Englishman Edward Dicey, a visiting acquaintance, noted only one change in their conversation, "an increased ardour for the war, a more intense sympathy for the cause in which the dead has fallen." Whether it was expressed in unreflective zeal or sober determination, the effect of a soldier's sacrifice on those left behind was significant.[50]

Whether it was a belief in regeneration through sacrifice, a pragmatic acceptance of death, or a belief in the individual's worth, the basic rightness of principles underyling the cause was a constant factor in shoring up support for the war. "We know now what War means," ruminated Oliver Wendell Holmes, Sr., in 1863, "and we cannot look its dull, dead ghastliness in the face unless we feel that there is some great and noble principle behind it." This was Charles Eliot Norton's cogent statement of those principles.[51]

This war is a struggle of the anti-democrats with the democrats; of the maintenance of the privilege of a class with the maintainers of the common rights of man. This view includes all the aspects of the war, and it is the ground upon which the people can be most readily brought to the sacrifices still required, and to the patient bearing of the long and heavy burdens it imposes upon them.

Belief in the transcendence of republican values also led Northerners to look deep inside themselves to explain the great suffering. They pondered the moral connection between victory, the cause, and the people conducting the conflict. If they were truly battling for noble principles, Ohio soldier John Stahl Peterson reasoned in an article, "if there are real issues of right and wrong involved in the contest, and we are in the right, we may rest assured that the results of a successful prosecution of the war will be worthy of all our sacrifices, and honorable to us as a people and nation." Northerners were convinced that they were fighting for the right principles and that victory was assured, despite repeated defeats and large numbers of casualties. Having the moral strength to endure the suffering enobled their character.[52]

But many Northerners wondered about the truth of this neat equation. If their war effort were based on eternal verities yet battlefield defeat was their lot then the character of the Northern people might be to blame. Thus, Northerners began to question their compliance with the slave oligarchy before Sumter and wondered if their battlefield losses were a punishment for allowing bondage to exist so long in a land of liberty. But this reasoning only led to further acceptance of battlefield suffering rather than to disillusionment with the war, for Northerners saw suffering as a way to redeem themselves. Oliver Edwards, a Massachusetts officer who indicated no abolitionist sentiments before the war, came to the conclusion that "our entire nation was responsible for slavery and protected it: we were all guilty, and were suffering a terrible blood atonement. The war would not end until slavery was sure to end with it." The New England abolitionist and literary figure Lydia Maria Child spoke in the same Mosaic tones. "If the war should last ten years we should not be punished more than we deserve."[53]

Charles Russell Lowell, a Massachusetts cavalry officer and nephew of the poet James Russell Lowell, agreed with Senator Charles Sumner about the inevitability of long, patient suffering. "He does not find in history any record of such great changes as we expect to see, having been brought about except with long wars and great suffering." Lowell did not believe that victory automatically attended a people who fought for a good cause. He knew that if they were not morally fit or had not "learned" from their suffering, victories would be wasted on them. Until the North developed more distinct ideas and policies "for a successful reorganization of the Southern territory and Southern institutions," it would not be prepared to eliminate the cause of the war—even if it won the conflict. For many, valuable goals inevitably demanded thought, suffering, and redemption of past sins.[54]

This conviction was a valuable antidote to the string of Northern defeats. Charles Eliot Norton called First Bull Run "a hard lesson, not . . . a disaster to be greatly regretted. . . . Everything that makes the attainment of our object in fighting more difficult, makes it at the same time more certain. Had we marched only to easy victory we might have had but half a triumph: *now* the triumph of our cause is likely to be complete." Norton had emancipation in mind, knowing that only repeated suffering would force the North to embrace it as a war measure. In addition, First Bull Run was a way for the Union to prove itself. "The test of defeat is the test of its national worth. Defeat shows whether it deserves success." Battlefield disaster would renew the war effort, destroy over-confidence, and act as the catalyst for a process of learning. If Northern supporters could not tolerate the emotional impact of losing on the field, the Union would be unable to win the war.[55]

To the great satisfaction of people like Norton, Unionists superbly met the test. They were able to do so by combining self-sacrifice with a dynamic commitment to ideals—a combination that sustained them through the nation's worst war. Joshua Chamberlain, a college professor from Maine, knew this as well as anyone. He commanded a regiment that played a crucial role in the battle of Gettysburg. Rising to division command because of his performance on Little Round Top, Chamberlain was given the honor of commanding the troops that formally accepted Lee's surrender at Appomattox. It was his firm belief that the horrors of battle were not strong enough to alter the Northern soldier's regard for the issues involved in the war. Men, he believed, "are made of mind and soul as well as body. We deal not only with exercises of the senses, but with deeper consciousness; affections, beliefs, ideals, conceptions of causes and effects, relations and analogies, and even conjectures of a possible order and organization different from what we experience in the present world of sense." The combatant and the civilian could endure the test of battle because of their ability to think beyond physical existence and their will to subordinate physical sensation to ideal. "Their life was not merely in their own experience but in larger sympathies," as Chamberlain put it. Because of their commitment to the principles of the war effort, Northerners were able to act for the good of others as well as for themselves; and they proved it by sustaining a bloody war for four years. William Wilkins Glenn, a despondent Rebel sympathizer in Maryland, admitted with a touch of admiration that the "cry of the 'Old Flag' and the 'Union' was a terrible power. The faith of the North in the progress of the country and of free institutions was even still greater."[56]

CHAPTER 4

Liberty and War

The vitality of ideology in mid-nineteenth-century America led Northerners to spend much time examining themselves, their military institutions, and their opponents in the context of those values. Midway through the war, one writer complained that the North had many journalists who were able to dig out news items but none who could capture what he defined as the human drama of the conflict: "an idea of the war, of what qualities it has developed in American citizens, of what kind of men our soldiers are, how they bear their trials, what they think, what they talk of, what they aim to do."[1] The writer need not have worried; for if the newspapers lacked this information, it was amply evident in the commentary of Northerners ranging from obscure soldiers to famous intellectuals. Their comments went beyond the writer's program, including thoughts on more than just the nation's solidiery. The result was a picture of their republican culture at war.

The war effort offered a serious challenge to the North's ideal of individualism because the necessity for communal action demanded a retreat from self-centered thought and action. How could a people so religiously committed to the development of the individual subordinate self to the country's needs? It was a question often asked by men and women who worried about the fitness of their people for engaging in war.

"I have always had a dream and theory about the virtues that are called out by war," reported Wilder Dwight, a perceptive, educated soldier from Massachusetts. "The calling . . . exacts very much from him [the soldier]. Self gets thrown into the background. It straggles out of the column, and is picked up, if at all, very late, by the rear-guard." Like Dwight, most people who posed the question came up with the right answer. His use of a military metaphor further illus-trated how readily they concluded that the nation's need was para-mount. "Self has to be put down more and more," agreed Emily Elizabeth Parsons, an obscure hospital volunteer, "and the work before us must take complete possession of our minds: this is not easy, but necessary." Likewise, Northerners readily concluded that avoidance of service was explained by selfishness. "They are wrapped up within themselves," thought New Yorker Thomas Owen of those who shirked their duty, "and care not how humanity progresses, so long as they enjoy freedom and the blessings somebody else has won for them."[2]

Few seem to have pondered the question of self versus the whole more seriously than did young Charles Russell Lowell, who was a Harvard graduate and an avid reader of transcendentalist literature. He had been highly concerned even before the war about balancing self-development, which he defined as mainly intellectual activity, and the social responsibility of contributing to the general welfare through practicing a trade or profession. This young intellectual found himself drawn by the pressures of the conflict to doubt the morality of the intellectual act in the midst of an event that called upon all the self-giving potential of each citizen. He began to judge others primarily by how much public spirit they expressed through their actions, and his optimism was hurt by the sight of army officers who let personal motives interfere with their public service. There were times when his fears led to extreme and pessimistic sentiments. "I feel every day more and more that a man has no right to himself at all," he wrote in the middle of 1863.[3]

On the other hand, Lowell developed a strong admiration for the model citizen engaged in war. To an old friend, he half-jokingly wrote: "I hope . . . that you are going to live like a plain Republican, mindful of the beauty and the duty of simplicity. . . . Don't grow rich; if you once begin, you will find it much more difficult to be a useful citizen." But the joking tone of his letter disappeared when Lowell wrote: "The useful citizen is a mighty unpretending hero. But we are not going to have any Country very long unless such heroism is developed. . . . being a soldier, it *does* seem to me that I should like nothing else so well as being a useful citizen." Lowell's republican model was his cousin John Murray Forbes. "How much he always manages to do in every direction without any previous preparation, simply by pitching in honestly and entirely," Charles wrote with admiration, "and I reflect that the great secret of doing, after all, is in seeing what is to be done."[4]

The same concern about self-development and its relation to the common good that Lowell pondered was also in Ralph Waldo Emerson's thoughts. Lowell's transcendentalist mentor believed that thought and action were mutually supportive. A republican people was a *thinking* as well as a virtuous people. Emerson wanted war to "bring out the genius of the men. In every company, in every town, I seek intellect & character." He sought men who could not only understand the issues of the war but who also had the heart to fight for them.[5]

Convinced that Northerners were capable of subordinating self to the whole, clergyman Samuel Osgood reminded the readers of a popular monthly magazine that it was the individual's duty to compromise personal will for a cause that was larger than any one person's life. The soldier, for example, had to give up his freedom and submit to army discipline, but it was a discipline that embodied the national will and mind. Thus his individualism was exalted, not crushed, in a combination of public law and private feeling. For the civilian, it was good to remember that "wherever our flag waves, it should be over families that mean to live not for self alone but for their neighbor, their country, and their race. For good or ill we must share in the common lot, and whether we live or die we do not belong to ourselves alone."[6]

Northerners considered the potential of their people for giving of self while not losing sight of individual worth. Transcendentalist David Wasson saw the war as a contest between base and noble impulses in man—that is, between the urge for self-power and the individual's willful submission to moral law. Civilization "makes liberty by making law"; therefore, a certain amount of force was necessary if ideal relations, "prescribed by reason, conscience, and reverence for the being of man," were threatened by people who allowed their animal-like drives to overpower their sense of the common good. Not surprisingly, Wasson saw the North as fighting on the side of the noble, civilizing principle and the South as representing the base principle. In his section, submission of self to the general good led to an elevation of each individual. "Here there is not only *community*, that is, the unity of many in the enjoyment of common privilege, but there is . . . a wide, manifold, infinitely precious evocation of intelligence, of moral power, and of all spiritual worth."[7]

Self-giving was a matter of self-control, and Northerners fully realized the significance of both concepts. Their self-image demanded a conviction that both attributes were characteristic of the North. Free institutions and self-government rested on the question of whether or not the Northern people could practice sufficient control to accept the war, its costs, and the disruptive issues it raised.

Many took the election of 1864 as a clear test of their fitness for self-government. For the first time in American history, a general election was held in the middle of a war. The Civil War was a conflict whose scope and intensity offered great temptation to forego politics as usual. Even aristrocrats such as Charles Francis Adams, Jr., were encouraged by "the faculty of a free *and intelligent* people to manage their own affairs," when he pondered the lesson to be learned from the election. Most of all, the canvass proved that republican government was strong enough to weather even the enormity of a civil war. As Lincoln put it soon after the election, "We can not have a free government without elections; and if the rebellion could force us to forego, or postpone a national election, it might fairly claim to have already conquered and ruined us." John Hay, Lincoln's private secretary, echoed the thoughts of more obscure Northerners when he saw in the election proof of "our worthiness of free institutions, and our capability of preserving them without running into anarchy or despotism."[8]

As a people, Northerners possessed enough self-control to sustain the delicate nature of free government in the nation's worst crisis. But the November election was not the last threat to their self-image. Lincoln's assassination, occurring at the war's end, aroused an enormously passionate response among prowar Northerners. Added to feelings of bitterness toward the South was the fact that for the first time a president had been murdered while in office. Thomas Owen's sorrow was almost overcome by feelings of revenge, "but that will not do. Now is the time we should control ourselves and look at things in their true light." Northerners saw in the election as well as in Lincoln's murder the potential for Northern society to slip into the kind of anarchy that had characterized the French Revolution; such confusion could be countered only by a firm command of passion. If free government were to be sustained, every Northerner had to say, "The 'law' *must* and *shall* be maintained, stand firm a little while and all will be well." After the passion of this horrible moment had passed, the threat to republican government would also pass.[9]

The war seemed to pose such a potent threat to republican self-control because Northerners realized that the fighting engendered strong passions. Armed conflict sprang from ominous, negative urges connected with the primordial nature of man. Francis Riddle, a former officer in one of the Union's black regiments, dwelled on war's evil origins in an address to veterans in 1886. "The spirit of war originates in sin. It feeds on hate, fattens on revenge, rejoices in cruelty, exults in ferocity, triumphs through oppression, outrages justice, reviles truth, stamps out generosity, and revels in villany." Yet Northerners also realized that even a free people sometimes had to resort to the use of military power to preserve order and sustain their cultural character. The citizen could engage in war without being soiled only if the fight were for a truly good cause. According to Riddle, it "is the spirit and motive of the soldier which give character to his calling, dignify his manhood, exalt his deeds, and make him a factor for good or evil in society."[10]

If the individual could understand the peculiar traits that characterized him and his society as exemplars of freedom and could maintain an awareness and devotion to those traits while in the army, the evil influences of war and military life would not change his character or threaten free government. In addition, such awareness and devotion would enoble military duty by turning it toward the preservation of liberty, rather than the oppression of freedom normally associated with standing armies in despotic lands.

Northerners worked hard to convince themselves that their army was truly representative of a free society. The Unitarian minister James Freeman Clarke was heartened by a trip to Washington, where he saw "an intelligent army of freemen, come to protect liberty and law. It is the nation itself which has taken up arms, and come to Washington to defend its own life and the ideas of the fathers."[11]

The structure of the Union military reinforced its closeness to society. The regular army, only sixteen thousand strong in 1861, retained an organization separate from the volunteer force. Regular officers were employed to command armies and corps (the highest field commands in the Union military), but the percentage of volunteer officers leading divisions and brigades increased as one scanned down the chain of command. Regiments, the basic building blocks of the armies, were rarely led by regulars, having been raised by local communities and officered early in the war by local notables elected by the rank and file. Although regular units served in the same field armies as volunteers, a distinction always existed between the two bodies. During the war, the regulars were reinforced by the enlistment of several thousand volunteers, who found that the harsh methods of instilling discipline still applied to them, as if they were of the same stamp as the "social outcasts" usually associated with regular service in peacetime.[12]

The volunteer army was truly what its name implied—a force of men who deliberately chose service. It was structured to remain separate from the regulars, with internal promotion providing experienced junior officers an opportunity to rise to field and staff positions in each regiment. Soldiers took pride in using the word "Volunteers" behind the number and state designations of their regiments. The distinction between them and the standing army was crucial; otherwise the Union's chief military power "would not have been the popular thing it was," believed Jacob Cox, one of the more competent volunteer generals of the war. The army's "close identification with the people's movement would have been weakened, and it, perhaps, would not so readily have melted again into the mass of the nation at the close of the war."[13]

Yet, retaining hold of republican traits, such as individualism, inevitably led to a clash between the code of obedience and the freedom of the citizen. This clash was the point of conflict between ideals of liberty and the principal tool of preserving the Union. It was part of a historic paradox. The values of American ideology were in conflict with all that military discipline implied. Before the Revolution, when the rhetoric of liberty was used to energize civilians to resist the use of

British regulars, it was easy to assert the irrefutable clash of freedom and military power. But now, when the nation was forced to use that same kind of military power to preserve its own liberty, it became much more difficult to arrive at a satisfying reconciliation of these two alien forces.

Northerners tried hard to do so. Like their Revolutionary ancestors, some expressed a belief that military professionalism was unnecessary for winning the war. They argued that spirit was the key to making a good warrior. "It does not require a well drilled soldier to fight well," asserted Frederick Pettit, a Pennsylvania infantryman. "All that is needed is plenty of courage, a good gun and ammunition for it, and I will insure the fight."[14]

Pettit took great liberty with the problem, for it was never that easy to reconcile the conflicting qualities of political freedom and military professionalism. Volunteers took their political lives into the army. Many officers could not forget that after the war their hopes for office rested with the very men they commanded, and too many of them coddled their subordinates. For the enlisted soldier, it was difficult to realize that those he had treated as equals in civilian life were now superior to him in the military pecking order. The free citizen suddenly found he had to adjust to an arbitrary system of government in which he had no voice.[15]

The army was filled with young men who had been raised in a culture that valued individual freedom. "Discipline of any kind, save that of public opinion, is unknown in the country," according to Charles Wainwright, a New York artilleryman of conservative leanings, "and contrary to the whole education and general habit of our people." As a result, "every man thinks that he is conferring a favour on the government by being here at all, and commences to pout and hang back so soon as government fails to furnish him with everything he is entitled to." Wainwright complained that officers, because they knew their military careers were temporary, often did not bother to learn how to properly fill out requisitions. Thomas Wentworth Higginson noted perceptively that the volunteers had a spirit that led them to fight and to die so magnificently that the public tended to overlook their deficiencies in other matters that impaired their usefulness as soldiers. Volunteers often paid scant attention to sanitation in camp, to proper preparation of food, and to the minutia of paperwork.[16]

The problem was, as Wilder Dwight accurately perceived, that "American soldiers will only become efficient in proportion as they abandon their national theories and give themselves up obediently to the *military laws* which have always governed the successful prosecution of war." Expressing the result more stridently than was necessary, Dwight believed the Union army was "crippled by the ideas of equality and independence which have colored the whole life of our people." Yet he touched the key solution when he wrote that a temporary retreat from individualism was called for, and that was a difficult choice for Northern citizens to make. However, Dwight felt they were intelligent enough to see its necessity.[17]

The result was a pragmatic truce between conflicting desire and need, but there never was a resolution of the antagonistic nature of liberty and the unthinking subordination of military life. Volunteer officers tried to find a "proper medium" between freedom and discipline. As citizen-soldiers learned the basic lessons of warfare with the same diligence they gave to their civilian jobs, officers more concerned with politics than efficiency were weeded out, and enlisted men learned by experience the need for arbitrary control. As Higginson put it, the men had to surrender for a time "the essential principle of the government."[18]

The advice of two noncommissioned officers spelled out how a *modus operandi* was developed. Charles Brush and Will Robinson, both of Illinois, drew on their experiences to offer tips to friends who had entered the army as officers. Discipline had to be instilled, they knew, "not harsh nor in an angry way, nor in an overbearing style." The officer had to "be kind and social and treat [his men] as brother soldiers fighting in the same great caus[e]." If officers saw to it that subordinates were properly supplied with food and clothing and kept their camps clean, they would follow "where ever they are led." The officer had to remember that each of his men had "sacrificed interests at home for the higher interest of patriotism." These were intelligent men, and the officer who showed them "proper consideration and confidence, receive it in return and consequently have that influence which insures the most perfect discipline."[19]

In short, the "best officers were those who, without sacrifice of dignity kept a lively sense of comradeship with their men." Mostly citizen-soldiers themselves, volunteer officers approached their tasks much as they did civilian jobs that involved the management of men. In fact, Jacob Cox found that men coming from professions such as civil engineering, railroad construction, and manufacturing made the best officers. The single most important qualification for a good officer was peacetime experience in "handling considerable bodies of men."[20]

This entente between freedom and discipline did not satisfy those who either complained about or tried hard to find a solution to the paradox of civil liberty and militarism. The *New York Times*, one of the strongest journalistic supporters of Northern war aims, criticized people who shortchanged military professionalism. Editors noted that, overly influenced by historic events such as the victory of Jackson's backwoodsmen over the British at New Orleans, Northerners "entered on the present war . . . convinced that the party which could put the largest number of men with muskets in the field at the outset of a contest was master of the situation." War, the newspaper warned, was a science "to be acquired and perfected by diligence, by perseverance, by time and by practice." No amount of spirit could substitute for a professional attitude. Another strong republican, cavalryman Nathan Webb of Maine, even wondered if it would not have been better in the long run if the country had gotten into an unjust war with Spain over Cuba in the 1850s. The nation would have learned the art of war then and could have used those lessons in the just and far more important conflict with the South.[21]

For the few who wished to see changes made in the nation's military system, there was the option of simply making it more free, while at the same time making it a bit more professional. A Navy lieutenant named Tecumseh Steece devoted a book to this problem. Tracing the history of the military and of social progress, he concluded that while society had developed free institutions the military remained the old despotic organization it had always been. The answer was to turn the military into a free institution itself, through the frequent election of officers by their men—"especially after great battles." By respecting the manhood of every soldier, the same virtue that made him a good citizen would make him a good soldier; thus, virtue would replace the subordination of one rank to another as the key to discipline. Steece recommended that the government establish a national academy to give civilians a more thorough military training than West Point offered and that graduates serve only a short time in the army and then return to civilian life before their morals and intellects could be perverted by their military service. This would put a large reserve of militarily trained—yet still virtuous—men in the population. They would be the nation's safeguard in case a large military force was needed. This scheme received the enthusiastic support of Ralph Waldo Emerson and several less well known writers.[22]

Steece and others like him sincerely believed that strengthening the militia system could provide the nation's military needs and safeguard freedom. Ironically, they inadvertently proved the futility of reconciling liberty and a professional army. Steece did not realize that his projected system was already in place, with many, if not most, West Point graduates returning to civilian life after graduation and with election of volunteer officers taking place, although on a much more limited scale than he envisioned. Steece simply proposed to invest citizen-soldiers with a greater degree of military education. The idea was not new to mid-nineteenth-century America, which had a system that already worked about as well as it could considering how incompatible were liberty and a professional military. If the militia system had not worked better by the 1860s and if the American people were not more willing to endure a military education, Steece's only hope was that the pressure of war might force them to consider the inadequacies and to work for change. But this hope was undercut by the working arrangement Northerners came to accept with the military. As long as they believed individualism did not drastically hurt the war effort, they would not question the wisdom of their military system. For better or worse, the North had achieved all it could in the struggle between the spirit of liberty and military subordination.

Yet, it would be wrong to shortchange that achievement. Despite the immense inefficiency, the volunteer army won the war. Citizen-soldiers developed a sense of professionalism, but it derived from experience and was quite different from the arbitrary, despotic discipline associated with regular armies. Looking back on his service with the 2nd Michigan Infantry, Henry Lyster recognized that the Spirit of '61 changed into something else by 1865. "The period of romance had changed to a period of system and endurance. . . . what was lost in enthusiasm and animation, was made up in concert of action and confidence in method." This sense of professionalism was strongly felt by those who volunteered in the 1862 call for troops, such as Ira Seymour Dodd of New Jersey. By then, he had few illusions about war and felt awe rather than jubilation when he joined. Dodd knew the army was a giant machine, and he was more willing than his predecessors to subordinate himself to its demands, to "be fitted" into it.[23]

Even after gaining experience, soldiers continued to view the relation between self and the military in uncertain terms. On the one hand, some believed the soldier kept most of his individualistic ideals. Thomas Livermore of New Hampshire recognized that education in civil life helped prepare a citizen to accept the self-discipline and respect for law that were necessary to be a good soldier. He grumbled but soon learned the value of discipline in camp and during battle. As a result, it "was not necessary to build up a mechanical habit of obedience in them." The citizen-soldier was a thinking individual, even in the middle of this large, impersonal force; he was not the automation republicans usually believed regular soldiers to be. Even after becoming professionals, volunteers obeyed an order "because it is reasonable," according to Thomas Wentworth Higginson, "not because it is an order." They applied a test of worth to each one. The practical military sense of Vermonters brigaded with Ira Seymour Dodd's regiment inspired him. In camp they had casual regard for discipline, but in battle—the crucial test—they strictly obeyed orders. "With all their independence and contempt for conventionalities," reasoned Dodd, "the discipline prevailing in that brigade was really most rigid." In short, just as the individual retained a strong sense of self in the social organization of civilian life, so did he give up only enough individual sovereignty in the army to insure military success. As Walter Carter of Massachusetts optimistically stated, "There is . . . an individuality in this crisis that belongs to everyone here, notwithstanding the gigantic vastness of the plan and general purpose."[24]

On the other hand, many soldiers could not be so certain of self in the army. Recognizing that discipline was necessary "sort of takes the manhood all out of a fellow," according to New Yorker George Metcalf. "It makes him a very small part of a very big complicated machine." These men used language that denoted submission, not compromise. Ira Seymour Dodd, who admired the rugged independence of his Vermont comrades, did not believe that his fellow Jerseymen fared so well. "The soul of the army, the mysterious solidarity of the mighty compelling organization, seemed to take possession of us; we knew that we were no longer our own." Abner Small wrote of the soldier's complete loss of individuality: "He no longer claims his enrolled name, he becomes simply an indistinguishable unit." The army melted individuality into a "composite—almost . . . a new type." At least regarding battle, if not regarding camplife, Dodd agreed with Small that military service merged the "individual consciousness into the composite consciousness of a regiment."[25]

Whether a soldier believed that the self could be retained intact, compromised, or lost in the war experience, his thoughts were overshadowed by the larger problem of how free people could bend their will to war without losing their individualism. The answer demanded a capacity for self-control. Citizens had to believe that they had enough self-possession to temporarily submit to military discipline without losing hold of their sense of independence.

In addition to developing positive views of themselves, Northerners engaged in fierce and widespread self-examination. They even questioned their belief in liberty and whether they had the moral stamina to preserve it.

The unexpected length and suffering of the war induced self-doubt about the North's prewar attitude toward slavery. Northerners widely questioned the morality of compromise with the slave power, believing now that it was tainted with the desire to place progress above patriotism. The language they used was almost self-flagellant. Before the war, clergyman Charles Edwards Lester asserted, Northerners "ran riot into every form of luxury and licentiousness which could tempt the appetite, exalt the pride, or influence the ambition." Critics began to believe that Northerners had taken free institutions for granted before the war, that they had been so obsessed with progress as to lose the vigilance necessary for the maintenance of free government, and that they had entrusted liberty to the hands of demagogues. Instead of a sincere desire to retain the national structure, the North now seemed to have been concerned only with maintaining, in Jane Grey Swisshelm's opinion, "the commercial copartnership of an organized band of man thieves and perjured traitors." However hard it may have been to admit their error, critics now believed that the prewar course of the North had been not only morally wrong but naive. "We had attempted an impossibility," Lester crowed. *"We had tried to make Liberty and Slavery live together in the same soil."*[26]

Northerners were paying a heavy price for their obsession with wealth. The lure of luxury submerged "purely patriotic feeling." New Yorker Maria Lydig Daly moaned when she thought of it. "Each man is out for himself; each one seeks how many dollars he can get out of his friends, his occupation, his place under the government." Many hoped the war would remind people that extravagance smothered the vigor of national spirit. "We are yet a nation of over grown babies," complained surgeon Robert Hubbard of the 17th Connecticut Infantry, "and . . . the fault is not so much one of nature as of education. We have had too much comfort & luxury and too little hard work and self denial." While recognizing the evil effects of luxury on their land, stout-hearted republicans hoped that it would not be fatal. But others realized the depth of suffering the nation could reach before it learned its lesson. Joseph Trego of the 5th Kansas Cavalry sarcastically predicted that Northerners would not oppose the slave power until it had assumed such a threat as to interrupt their concentration while "in the act of counting money or reckoning up an account."[27]

The surest indication of moral failure was in not realizing before Sumter that slavery was the greatest enemy of liberty. Even as the Union struggled for its existence, slavery affected the thinking of its champions. Lydia Maria Child worried that the war might be lost because of Lincoln's concern for safeguarding bondage in the border states, even as he declared emancipation in Confederate territory. She was grateful for the Proclamation but saddened that it was done "reluctantly and stintedly." Lincoln's policy lacked " a halo of moral glory. This war has furnished many instances of *individual* nobility, but our *national* record is mean." [28]

In addition to the enervation of prosperity and a grudging attitude toward abolition, politicians seemed to threaten the Northern self-image. Men who could not give up partisanship were highly visible in the news media and were the objects of disgusted commentary. They seemed to work for the triumph of the South by fracturing Northern unity, or at the very least they worked for personal advancement at a time when the nation needed the selfless aid of all its citizens. Henry Smith of the 26th Michigan Infantry expressed the bitterness felt by those who risked their lives for such an ignoble set of men. Are we to suffer, he asked, "while these perjured vampyres [sic] are quarrelling and bickering over the spoils of office—holding up the bugbear of *party* loss, while blood and tears are vainly striving to maintain the cause of the Union?"[29]

Army administration seemed no less open to criticism. The largest bureaucracy yet seen in America, it inevitably became a refuge for incompetent as well as unscrupulous men in the middle and higher ranks of authority. Seeing the wickedness of supposedly virtuous soldiers made Ohio cavalryman Thomas Covert shudder with despair. "I don't know but all armies are so, but I did not used to think so of our army, in the old revolutionary times by reading of it. Our officers from the highest to the lowest are more than half of them thieves." The pomp of military life—the color, shine, and choreographed ceremony that valued outward appearance at the expense of inner morality—was a source of decadence, which ill fitted a republican people. Daniel Bond of Minnesota felt depressed when he saw Northerners fawning over the badges of martial glory like children over candy. From reading Plutarch, he believed that a soldier was a man who despised luxury and show; yet he saw how men valued them in the army. He began to doubt that Northerners had the moral stamina needed for freedom, and he knew that if people were not worthy of liberty they would not retain it.[30]

Strong supporters of the war also saw moral weakness in the Northern spirit when they measured the extent to which society felt the war. In the beginning, Emerson believed the conflict affected all aspects of Northern life, which was probably a reflection of how the war influenced his own spirit rather than the nation's. Yet in 1862 he concluded that Northern spirit was far from focused on the war. Trade and entertainment took precedence, and Emerson sarcastically suggested the government transfer the war's prosecution to private enterprise. "Let Adams's Express undertake by contract the capture of Richmond, of Charleston, of the pirate Alabama." If not that, simply let England or France intervene and the government undoubtedly would make haste to seize the major commercial ports of the South in order to monopolize European trade, while the Union might remain fragmented.[31]

For Emerson and other critics, this denoted a lack of moral fiber that could harm the war effort. The emotions of Northern society had to be in tune with the army; self-sacrifice on the battlefield would lead only to partial victory if civilians were more concerned with money and comfort than with the war. Walt Whitman realized this every time he visited Brooklyn and sensed the unreality of civilian life compared to his work in the hospitals. The constant round of gayety, big dinners, and entertainments contrasted sharply with the suffering and "bread & molasses for supper" that the sick and injured endured. It seemed to him "very flippant & shallow somehow." The gloomy summer of 1864, with its military stalemates in Virginia and Georgia, seemed to mark the nadir of vigilance. "The war sentiment among the people of the North appears to be at its lowest ebb," moaned James Connolly, an officer in Sherman's army, "everybody is either scrambling for wealth or for office, and giving only an occasional thought to the soldiers in the field, just about as the Southern planters used to think of their slaves, toiling in the cotton and the cane."[32]

Finally, the immense fraud that attended the war effort, inevitable in any huge undertaking by the government, hit home for those Northerners who firmly believed in their potential for good. "Selfishness, alas! in the forms of personal ambition, and the cursed greed of gain, are found hanging like vampyres [sic] upon the throat of the best enterprises," cried Horace James, a Massachusetts chaplain. There were many in the North whose awareness of republican values was apparently almost nonexistent, whose aspirations for right-living were null, and whose patriotism was untouched by feelings of duty to anyone but themselves. As a result, they made "merchandise of a distressed and perplexed nation."[33]

Henry Olcott, appointed special commissioner by the War and Navy Departments to root out and prosecute fraudulent government contractors, waded neck-deep into a morass of corruption. "For one pound of necessary metals, one yard of fabric, one gallon of liquid, the price of two was paid. Our soldiers were given guns that would not shoot, powder that would only half explode, shoes of which the soles were filled with shavings, hats that dissolved often in a month's showers, and clothing made of old cloth, ground up and fabricated over again." He estimated from his long and intimate experience that as much as twenty-five percent of all war-related government expenditures "were tainted with fraud." That amounted to over seven hundred million dollars paid to criminals or simply wasted. Honest and patriotic businessmen told Olcott they simply gave up trying to do business with the government because they could not do so without being underbid by unscrupulous men.[34]

But war-related immorality was not confined to the counting house. Frederick Cook, a typesetter in Chicago, recalled in his memoirs the effect war had on that city's social life and moral tone. The calls for troops dug deeply into the solid, dependable elements of the population, which "tended to weaken the defences that make for continence." Unmarried soldiers home on leave with a devil-may-care attitude, their pockets stuffed with greenbacks, tore up the town. Gamblers flocked to Chicago to ply their trade and openly spout Southern sympathies, while "war-widows" turned to prostitution and bounty-jumpers made a mockery of recruitment efforts. Cook especially remembered the brothel of a man named Roger Plant, whose motto seemed to epitomize the breakdown of self-control among Chicago's urban dwellers. Gilded on blue shades that decorated every window of the place, it flared the unanswerable question: "Why Not?" Writing in 1910, Cook bitterly concluded: "At this distance the war time is apt to be regarded as one of heroisms only. Yet it was the seamy and sordid side—the face distorted by lust and passion—that most insistently forced itself on the observer's attention."[35]

It was true, as Jane Grey Swisshelm noted, that there was "a large abundance of sublime courage, virtue and patriotism in the people"; but it coexisted with much chicanery, selfishness, and debauchery as well. She wondered if Northern society was not like a quartz boulder, "which must be ground to powder in order to secure and preserve the gold scattered through and imbedded in it."[36] Many Northerners saw the war itself as that grinding, refining agent. Questions regarding the moral strength of the people were answered by the Northern decision to go to war in 1861. That act and sustaining the war effort despite its horrible bloodletting proved to Northerners that their people could be prosperous and virtuous at the same time. The war effort itself confirmed their republican self-image by proving they retained a healthy awareness of the common good and a willingness to sacrifice personal comfort for the nation that was akin to the patriotism displayed by the Revolutionary generation.

Oliver Wendel Holmes, Sr., used a unique and apt metaphor for this, comparing the perceived demise of patriotism before 1861 with the sinking of a drowned body. Just as cannon fire over the water brought up the body so did the artillery fire at Fort Sumter bring to the fore latent morality. "The bravery of our free working-people was overlaid, not smothered," Holmes argued, "sunken, but not drowned." Stimulated, Northerners would employ the same energies to defeat the Confederacy that they had used to build a prosperous society. "War *has* taught us, as nothing else could, what we can be and are. It has exalted our manhood and our womanhood, and driven us all back upon our substantial human qualities, for a long time more or less kept out of sight by the spirit of commerce."[37]

Many other people found encouragement in the fact that accepting the need for war was a step toward moral redemption. "Our best ground of hope now," wrote Emerson, "is in the healthy sentiment which appears in reasonable people all over the country, accepting sacrifices, but meaning riddance from slavery, & from Southern domination." Criticism had an inherent power for positive ends; voicing it was cathartic for people troubled by doubts and evidence of moral laxity. It also strengthened the urge for self-denial, which helped them to accept suffering. Those who believed Northerners had been remiss before 1861 could absorb much punishment to atone for their error. Arthur B. Carpenter, a young and fervent supporter of the war from Indianapolis, argued that a five- or ten-year war would be just retribution for the Northern people. It would eliminate the "filth and dead heads" of the nation, allowing Americans to try their "luck at sustaining a republican government for 80 or 90 years again."[38]

The war also spurred some Northerners to examine more sharply than before the nature of morality. Sergeant Jonathan P. Stowe of Massachusetts knew that the army was a good laboratory for studying human nature. What he saw confirmed his notion "that we do not the *right* for the *love* of *right* but simply because society demands it and we all *feel it and know it*." Unfortunately, "like a set of hypocrites . . . we . . . pretend to be better citizens in doing what is virtuous and just than we really are or ever will be unless we adopt the quaker doctrine of doing right for rights sake." Emerson argued that the virtue displayed in the war largely resulted from the antithetical example of the enemy. "Their perversity is still forcing us into better position than we had taken," he critically charged. "Their crimes force us into virtues to antagonize them and we are driven into principles by their abnegation of them." Holmes, who always seemed to have something worthwhile to say about his society's attitude toward the conflict, shrewdly observed that war asked much of the individual Northerner but did not necessarily ask him to give up everything he possessed. The potential for complete self-sacrifice existed, of course, in the exposure to bullets on the battlefield, but that was the result of a throw of the dice. What the war demanded immediately was the sacrifice of luxury, time, and the willingness to risk all else if chance desired it.[39]

What Stowe, Emerson, and Holmes were getting at was a frankly realistic attitude toward virtue. Morality did not divinely spring from some part of man's nature that was untouched by the life around him, but was influenced by a variety of factors—by the social mores of his culture, by the bad example of his enemies, or by the self-interested knowledge that he could engage in a virtuous act without necessarily losing all that he held dear. Alexis de Tocqueville, another insightful observer of Northern society, believed that the citizens of a democracy would agree to conduct a war only if it reached such proportions as to disturb commercial pursuits. They would then turn their commercial energies to the prosecution of war in order to restore the peace needed for good business. The mere fact that it took a war—as so many Northerners asserted—to bring the people back to a keen awareness of virtue is proof that influences from the world surrounding the individual were vitally important in virtuous conduct.[40]

That virtue should originate in something other than a pure regard for the right was consistent with Tocqueville's definition of American democracy. He believed that individuals would more readily act in a moral way if they were convinced that their actions were right not only by the standards of some independent moral code but by being beneficial to them as well. Selflessness and self-interest seemed to come together in the war the minute the slave power launched an attack on free institutions, for that made defense of the Northern way of life a war against a power built on black slavery. Of course, few delved so deeply or honestly into the nature of virtue as did Emerson or Tocqueville. Most were content to remain on a relatively superficial plane and accepted the war experience as marvelous proof of their morality. Many were also excited by the possibility of self-less action and the undeniable fact that the possibility had become a reality in hundreds of thousands of individual cases.

Virtue, in short, was malleable; it was subject to the right influences. In the 1860s Northerners were convinced that the war was the greatest possible cultivator of individual and civic morality. One way it achieved this result was to bring people's awareness back to basics and to teach them the beauty of simplicity and the evil of extravagance. Emerson saw war as cutting through "letter & form" down to the "roots of strength in the people." He ascribed to a long-held view that character would be manifested in communication and appearance—a coherence of inner worth and outer persona. In war, "everybody . . . drops much of brag & pretension, & shortens his speeches. The fop in the street, the beau at the ball feels the war in the air . . . & becomes modest & serious. The writer is less florid, the wit is less fantastical. The epicure & the man of pleasure put some check & cover on their amusements." Likewise, professions that stuck to the basics remained strong in the dissonance of war time. For example, baking, butchering, farming, and wood chopping remained essential; but "coach painting & bronze matchholders" were ephemeral. The demands of war and the strength of virtue came together in Charles Russell Lowell's advice to his fiancée to prepare herself for a long war. "For years to come, I think all our lives will have to be more or less solderly,—i.e. simple and unsettled; simple because unsettled."[41]

The nation's leaders seemed to epitomize virtue. Holmes was much impressed after meeting Grant. "I doubt if we have had any ideal so completely realized as that of the republican soldier in him," which for Holmes meant the "entire loss of selfhood in a great aim." Grant also reminded Lydia Maria Child of Garibaldi, "in his courage, promptness, energy, and presence of mind; in the brevity and good sense of his letters; in the simplicity of his manners, his aversion to being lionized." In Lincoln's writings appeared evidence of his strong commitment to what Charles Eliot Norton called "the possibility of the coexistence of a strong government with entire and immediate dependence upon and direct appeal to the people.[42]

It was equally important that rank-and-file members of the army exemplify morality. Northerners realized what it took to make a republican army. "I know that it will require a great deal of moral and mental training to make a good Soldier of me," reasoned Sanford Truesdell of New York. A desire to infuse "a high tone of character" into the volunteer force was as important in prompting Thomas Wentworth Higginson to enlist as was his antislavery motive. Anything less than soldiers who were "brave in action, undaunted in spirit, unwearied in energy but patient of discipline, self-controlled, and forbearing," in the words of Charles Eliot Norton, would be a denial of their culture's influence on the character of their citizens. Military automatons could win battles, but it took men "who know for what and why they are fighting" to win a cause such as the Union's.[43]

An Ohio officer wrote a set of resolutions calling on all soldiers to reflect the holiness of their cause by not swearing or complaining, and by keeping themselves in good health while diligently learning the art of war. In Unionist eyes, the Northern soldier was unique because of the uniqueness of the institutions that nurtured him. The Russian immigrant Nadine Turchin found confirmation of this in the Army of the Cumberland's silent suffering due to food shortages in Chattanooga. "A citizen-soldier who feels free by his birthright endures all these things because he does not feel obliged to endure them," she wrote. "He has volunteered to serve for the love of liberty . . . and he accepts the consequences with the firmness of a stoic." Walt Whitman often reiterated this theme in his letters and writing. "Any thing like beggars or deceivers, are very rare," he wrote to a friend. "The soldiers are nearly altogether young American men of decent breeding, farmers' sons ordinarily educated, but well behaved and their young hearts full of manliness & candor." In the backward glance of a veteran who dwelled on the common soldier of the Civil War, it was an army of "moral, Christian, manly men" that protected liberty.[44]

The best of the Union soldiers were the "thinking bayonets" autocratic rulers dreaded to have in their armies; they were republicans who fought for communal purposes in which they believed. "It is 'thinking' that inspired those bayonets," wrote an anonymous pamphleteer, "and it is because they are in the grasp of thinking men that they were clothed with all their majesty and power." As long as the military consisted of men who "in becoming *soldiers* . . . did not cease to be *citizens*," the armed might of the Union would remain an army of intelligent freemen. After the war, veteran Charles Mackenzie believed that the Federal military could hardly have been called an army at all, but rather "a voluntary association" banded together at the men's free will "for mutual protection, advancement and profit." Their aim was to preserve their "property"—the government. The Union soldier was not a machine, as were those who followed Frederick the Great or Napoleon; he was a citizen whose failure in the field meant the loss of all private and public liberties.[45]

Nowhere was the theme of the virtuous soldier more persistent than in the idea that wounded Federals bore their suffering like true men. Observers asserted that injured men maintained self-control as long as they were conscious; only when delirium set in did they groan and cry. Wounded men seemed easier to care for than sick soldiers because the former had made their sacrifice in direct contact with the enemy. Elvira Powers, a volunteer in one of Nashville's hospitals, met a sick soldier who was very despondent, "for I enlisted to *fight*, not to be *sick!*" he told her. When asked if he did not suffer for the Union as much as a wounded man, "a quick flash of the eye, a smile and an emphatic '*no*,' tell us that it is entirely a new thought." Ill soldiers had "a hopeless, disheartened expression," as Delaware resident Anna Ferris put it after seeing trainloads of men being sent to Northern hospitals, while the wounded appeared "cheerful."[46]

The influence of free institutions on character was further demonstrated in the belief that soldiers could return uncorrupted to civilian society. A Missouri cavalry commander's farewell address to his regiment stressed this notion. "By your conduct cast the lie in the teeth of those who have said that the soldiers were become corrupt and demoralized," he ordered his men. "Show them that you are better citizens for having been good soldiers; that you have learned a lesson of orderly obedience to law and faithful discharge of duty which the cowardly shirks who have slandered you would do well to learn from you."[47]

The officer could so confidently predict the immediate future because he knew that the army had drawn a portion of the solid foundation of society into its ranks. This knowledge not only shored up confidence in the military's ability to disappear into civilian life after the conflict, but also gave hope in the war's darkest hours. The army had a solid heart of dependable men, who made up the same core of resiliency in society. Despite poor generalship, Charles Francis Adams, Jr., did not despair for the Army of the Potomac, for "all underneath is so sound and good."[48]

Likewise, Northerners saw the same kind of people as the social foundation for their war effort. One of their most inspiring themes was Southern denigration of Northern laborers as mudsills and industrial slaves. Incensed by Southern aristocratic claims "that they were a noble-blooded and we a mean-spirited people; that they ruled the country by their better pluck, and if we did not submit they would whip us by their better courage," many soldiers joined the army to prove that working men could understand and act on weighty questions of polity. Lincoln thought working people had a special interest in opposing the rebellion, for they realized this was "a war upon the rights of all working people" to enjoy the results of their own labor. Northerners considered the middle and working classes to be conservative, or in the words of New York City businessman Robert Ogden, holding a sentiment "that is intelligent, that runs between extremes, that is true, loyal, and patriotic, and that will govern for the right." Their careful, informed thinking was "sound on the war question." Even members of the New England elite, such as Thomas Wentworth Higginson, were encouraged by news that the middle ranks of society were loyal in turbulent Baltimore, while the gentry and the lower class sympathized with the South.[49]

Such views helped to explain why Northerners did not fear a military coup. They recognized the possible dangers an army could pose to freedom, especially during a time of dissatisfaction with the civil government's conduct of the war. The greatest danger was that the people would consent to a military dictatorship to bring the conflict to an end, motivated by their dissatisfaction with the lack of vigorous

prosecution of the war. The adoption of increasingly radical war policies by the Lincoln administration undercut this danger. Also important in soothing the fear of a military government was the belief, as
stated by Oliver Wendell Holmes, Sr., that "the army is only the
representative of a self-governing community. This army is not like to
enslave itself or the families it comes from, to please the leader whom
it trusts for an emergency. The pilot is absolute while the vessel is
coming into harbor, but the crew are not afraid of his remaining master
of the ship." Lincoln expressed his confidence in civil authority when
he appointed Joseph Hooker as commander of the Army of the Potomac. He had heard of Hooker's belief that the government needed an
absolute leader. "Of course it was not *for* this, but in spite of it, that I
have given you the command. Only those generals who gain suc-
cesses," Lincoln continued with some sarcasm, "can set up dictator-
ships. What I now ask of you is military success, and I will risk the
dictatorship."[50]

While convinced of their own character—as individuals and as a
people—Northerners reversed the image of virtue when pondering the
nature of their enemies. Working within the context of their values,
they pictured the Confederacy as the antithesis of everything associated with their own ideology. They saw justification for their war
upon slavery in the conduct of the Rebel war effort, in the social
attitudes of Southerners, and even in the personal characteristics of
individual Confederates.

In contrast to free, thinking republicans, Southerners seemed ignorant and misguided by their leaders. Luther C. Furst, a soldier in a
Pennsylvania regiment, described civilians on Virginia's peninsula as
"scarcely above the slave," with "no idea of the cause of the war or
what they are fighting for." Northerners often conversed with captured or wounded Rebels and found their opponents had mistaken
ideas about the Union's war aims. Fire-eaters and prejudice against the
North had led them to believe that extermination of white Southerners
and exaltation of Negroes were Northern goals. Wounded Rebel prisoners at Gettysburg believed they had fought to preserve Southern
freedom from Northern aggression. They had trouble understanding
the reasons for Northern fighting when their captors explained them
and were "staggered indeed" but not quite comprehending when hos-

pital volunteer John Foster explained that the tendency in Southern society was toward the denial of popular liberty by a privileged aristocracy. Logically, Unionists concluded that "the rebellion was never the expression of the common people."[51]

For Unionists, the appearance and behavior of the Rebels denoted inferiority. Soldiers noted the sallow, often gaunt look of Confederates and contrasted it with the healthy glow of Union warriors. Henry Dwight of Ohio was disgusted with the "long uncombed hair" and "butternut colored homespun clothes" of the Rebel prisoners he guarded. A New Hampshire private, John Burrill, thought anyone who could look upon such a "miserable lot of men" and still excuse the rebellion was less than a man. Wounded Rebels who fell into Union hands seemed to bear their suffering less manfully than did Federals. Without doubt, the treatment of captured Yankees by the Confederates became a source of bitter hatred for the North. Nothing else so vividly illustrated the difference between his section and the South, believed Wisconsin soldier Harvey Reid after being released from Rebel prisons. He was overjoyed to be "once more in a land where . . . man is treated as man, and is not supposed to lose his humanity and human feelings by becoming a soldier."[52]

Unquestionably, this image of the South was skewed and ungenerous. Northern attitudes were guided by cultural values, by the natural tendency of belligerents to view their enemy as morally inferior, by their limited contact with selected Rebels, and by imperfect knowledge of Confederate policies. At least one Union soldier, Theodore Lyman of Meade's staff, realized the popular image was erroneous and believed there was "no shadow of doubt that the body of the Southerners are as honestly, as earnestly and as religiously interested in this war as the body of Northerners." He also realized how difficult this was for his countrymen to believe. "Of course such sentiments in the North are met with a storm of 'Oh! How *can* they be?'—'That is morally impossible'—'No one *could* really believe in such a cause!' Nevertheless there is the fact."[53]

This image of the South reinforced Northerners' image of themselves as the guardians of liberty in America. It also offered Unionists a way to justify their opposition to the South's self proclaimed right to revolt—a right that was an important part of the American heritage.

If one viewed the Confederacy as an unnatural revolution engineered by a conspiracy of slaveholders against the will and interests of a majority of the south's solid citizens, the inconsistency disappeared. The Confederacy's aim was not to promote free institutions but to insure the survival of human bondage. As Lincoln explained it, the rebellion was a "wicked exercize [sic] of physical power," which was incompatible with the revolutionary heritage. "What form of *liberty and free institutions* is to be *reconstructed*," a Chicago editor incredulously thundered, "when the corner-stone of its constitution blazes with the lurid, revolting glare of SLAVERY?"[54]

A Confederate prisoner captured at Gettysburg who wrote his memoirs under the improbable name Decimus et Ultimus Barziza offered a pointed critique of Northerners' attitudes about themselves. He repeatedly talked with his captors, engaging in debates that would have impressed the great lawyer and orator Daniel Webster. "Verily, this is a peculiar people," Barziza wrote in 1865, before the bitterness of the war had subsided. "They are extremely bigoted, and actually bloated with self-love. They think everything of their's is better than anybody else's; their religion purer; their men braver, and women fairer; their country better; their manners and customs more enlightened, and their intelligence and culture immeasurably superior." Ego inflation like this was wormwood and gall to a prisoner demoralized by his lot and afraid for his health in cold Northern prison pens. But it was exalting to Unionists who felt the power of republican morality. They knew what Connecticut lawyer Francis Wayland meant when he wrote: "The success of our republican institutions must depend on the morality and intelligence of the citizens." The war for the Union was *the* supreme trial of those virtues. Joshua Chamberlain argued that it would "test and finally determine the character of the interior constitution and real organic life of this great people."[55]

CHAPTER 5

White Dissent, Black Freedom

The size and scope of the Northern war effort bred a series of radical policies, adopted by the Lincoln government, that threatened the self-image Northerners had energetically created. Federally sponsored emancipation, military conscription, confiscation of private property, and violation of civil rights were used by the government to meet the demands of the war. These policies were temptations to abuse the delicate nature of free institutions, yet were fervently supported by people who deeply believed in liberty. The North's concept of liberty proved, however, to be dynamic and flexible enough to accommodate this paradox. In the process, the Northern consciousness began admitting the concept of black freedom in what had previously been an all-white structure of liberty. Questions involving emancipation, adherence to the law in adopting war policies, and public self-control split the North, making the Civil War the most divisive war effort in American history.

These nearly fatal questions of policy were not at issue for the first year of the war. During that time, there was a solid consensus in favor of the war. Goals were enunciated and policies set that were so basic and safe as to enlist the support of all factions. The war was fought to reestablish the legitimate authority of the Federal government, thereby preserving the free institutions important in Northern minds. The goal was not yet to transform Southern society by eliminating slavery or the Southern aristocracy, despite the fact that Northerners believed early on that those two elements had started the war. Northerners had developed a static conception of the Union before 1861, accepting as a given the existence of slavery in the South alongside freedom in the North. Moreover, they were bothered by the government's lack of explicit authority to abolish slavery. Many Northerners liked to point out that it took a long time for the solid middle ranks of society to loosen their hold on one idea and fasten upon another. Thus the war was strictly a preservationist conflict; the primary goal of safeguarding the status quo was expressed in a conservative fashion.[1]

The military policies adopted by Lincoln's army reflected this conservatism. Orders were issued to safeguard the property of those in the occupied territory who did not support the rebellion, and strategic arrangements were made to defeat the Confederacy with the least amount of bloodshed. It was hoped that a sharp tactical and strategic defeat or perhaps a series of such defeats would convince the Rebels that they could not militarily win their cause. It was hoped that the Confederates would then be prompted to agree to terms that would enable them to reenter the Union with slavery intact. Generals Winfield Scott, George B. McClellan, and Don Carlos Buell of the Union army proceeded to plan and implement conservative military policies.[2]

If the war had been the short, relatively easy conflict so many had wanted, these conservative goals and the safe means to achieve them probably would have worked. Unfortunately, to the surprise, dismay, and even horror of both sides, the war began to assume gigantic proportions. Northerners grossly underestimated the number of troops, the amount of time, and the expenditure of money and lives needed to subdue a determined, resilient people covering a wide expanse of geographically diverse territory. They underestimated the Southern will to resist, believing there existed large segments of Unionist sentiment throughout the Confederacy. Beginning with Fort Henry and Fort Donelson in February 1862, a string of significant Union victories seemed to confirm the wisdom of their conservative policies, as the Federal armies struck deep into the heart of the Confederacy. But the horrible losses of the war's first great bloodbath at Shiloh, the devastating failure of McClellan's Peninsular campaign by early July, and a Confederate invasion of Union-occupied Kentucky in August proved how futile was their hope for a short, relatively painless war.[3]

The summer of 1862 saw the abandonment of conservative goals and means and the destruction of the consensus built upon them. In September, Lincoln rescinded the writ of *habeas corpus* for persons arrested on suspicion of interfering with army enlistments or aiding the rebellion in any other way. Immediately thereafter, the secretary of war established a system of provost marshals throughout the nation, with agents in each state assigned the task of arresting deserters as well as civilians charged by the military with disloyalty. These agents were given wide powers to root out all enemies of the war effort, from common thieves who stole government property to Confederate spies, and could call on the aid of military forces as well as the civil police. As a result, an estimated fifteen thousand Northerners were held without due process for suspicion of antiwar sentiments and actions.[4]

In July the second and most powerful act to confiscate the property of rebels was enacted and signed by Lincoln. The earlier act, passed in August 1861, had little impact on the war because its provisions were too lax and because the public mood was not yet ripe for vigorous confiscation. While the first act affected only those Rebels caught in the act of resisting the government, the second act authorized the confiscation of all property belonging to known Rebels—including, irrevocably, their slaves. The aim was to strike at the backbone of Confederate power—property, cotton, and slaves—and to use these resources for the benefit of the Union armies.[5]

The most radical policy change for the Northern government was conversion from antiabolition to an emancipationist course. This new policy was more hotly debated and denounced than any other; conversely, the policy was more strongly supported by those who remained avid supporters of the war. Suspension of the writ of *habeas corpus* gave far more power to a military government than theory warranted. The confiscation of personal property was a direct blow to the individual's right of ownership; and Lincoln's Preliminary Emancipation Proclamation, issued on September 22, flew in the face of all legal and political precedent. The Constitution failed to speak about the Federal government's authority to abolish slavery—the most convincing argument was that it reserved the right to own human property to the state level. The Federal government did not hold a clear legal mandate to interfere with that right. Many Unionists were appalled at Lincoln's alteration of the founding fathers' handiwork. It incensed them even further that by a stroke of the pen he had transformed the war for the Union into an abolitionist war.[6]

These radical policies altered the goals of the war, as well as the means of achieving them. However, the primary purpose—the preservation of free institutions—remained the same. Even those who criticized the new policies remained faithful to that basic purpose, although they rejected the process by which this purpose was to be achieved as being ideologically unsound. The Union now sought to win the war by destroying the institution of slavery itself and the aristocracy based on it. The government sought to prosecute the conflict by restricting personal freedoms in the North. Those freedoms seemed in greater jeopardy in March 1863, when the government instituted a nationwide draft to coerce men into the army. For a people weaned on the voluntarism that was the heritage of the Revolution, this step was seen as personally insulting as well as dangerous to individual liberty.[7]

Northern critics of the war, as we now know, were a diverse group. There were peace-at-any-price men, active supporters of the military effort who also felt free to criticize Lincoln's policies, and people who fell somewhere between those extremes. In the minds of contemporary Northerners who supported the vigorous measures, they were all cut from the same cloth—a traitor's cloak. Members of the vigorous consensus called all dissenters "Copperheads"; thus, they willfully ignored the diversity of the dissenters' opinions and their yearning to be considered for what they were—a loyal opposition. Despite contemporary opinion, most dissenters were united by two things: sincere support for the maintenance of the Union and their ideologically motivated criticism of Lincoln's policies.[8]

Many dissenters argued that the Union could not be restored by conquest. Coercion would lead to nothing but despotism, for it denied the free will of the governed. Both the North and South had to mutually agree if a union of the sections was to have any hope of success.[9]

Inevitably, the dissenters were charged with being part of a conspiracy. Those who subscribed to this theory charged that the abolitionists had gained control of the Northern war effort. They also believed that radicals had manipulated the government toward their own political goals—emancipation and the breakup of the Southern aristocracy—and in the process had abandoned free institutions in the North. "I look upon secession and abolition as twin brothers," declared John Davis, a West Virginia politician, for those who practiced both were insensitive to the fragile nature of republicanism. Critics believed the nation's only hope lay in those conservatives who "have worshipped at the pure Shrine of the Government of their pure, wise revolutionary fathers," as Kentuckian Charles Wintersmith put it, and who were sworn to protect the constitution as it had always been interpreted. The radical war was not being fought for the good of the whole nation but for the satisfaction of a clique.[10]

Dissenters were conservative, to say the least, in their attitudes toward emancipation. They feared it would drive out all hope of conciliating the Rebels, believing emancipation proved to the enemy that disregard for constitutional law was an important part of the Northern war effort. Radicals, "one-idea men," were sacrificing not only the unity of America but thousands of young men as well, many of whom resented having the goals of the war changed in midstream. Dissenters did not see slavery as a moral evil—at least not a moral evil whose destruction lay in the means of politics or war. Although realizing that the rebellion was based on slavery, dissenters were hobbled by what they took to be constitutional restraints on federal action. However slavery might die, and dissenters rarely speculated on that possibility except to vaguely assert that it would self-destruct under the pressures of war, it would be improper to eliminate it unconstitutionally.[11]

Ironically, despite their continued belief in the war's basic purpose, critics of the war policies were in one way more closely related to their Southern neighbors than to their radical Northern neighbors. Dissenters tended to be Democrats, while the political focus of the radical policies was Republican. Here was the most visible line of demarcation, and it is not surprising that vigorous prosecutors tended to label all Democrats, however erroneously, as traitors. Dissenters often spoke of their views in much the same way as did Southerners. In Connecticut, for example, critics of the war policies self-consciously made the connection between their concern for individual liberties, states' rights, and a modest and unobtrusive central government with the South's success. C. Chauncey Burr, the editor of a dissenting newspaper in New York City, openly proclaimed the Confederacy to be closer to the founding fathers in its attitudes than was Lincoln's government. Across the country in rural Iowa, Charles Mason worked hard to convince his fellow citizens that conservative, even Southern, visions of the Union were correct.[12]

Not all dissenters self-consciously held up the South as a model. More commonly, they revealed their Southern affinity by elaborating on their concerns. Critics feared the trend toward centralization of government. While they denounced the extreme states' rights view they found a powerful central government to be equally distasteful. Like their Southern neighbors, dissenters favored a strict reading of the Constitution, viewing it as a "formal set of rules, not, as Republicans would have it, a living document that incorporated laws, customs, and practices." Dissenters placed great emphasis on respecting the constitutional-legal structure to the letter.[13]

The ideological division of the North was in some ways blatant, in other ways subtle. Clearly, dissenting Democrats were more closely aligned with many Southern views: in their adherence to strict construction of the Constitution, in their closer affinity to the world of the founding fathers, and in their fear of centralized government. Yet they were far from aristocratic or hierarchical in their attitude toward liberty. They believed in the free-market economy, in competition, in opportunity for middle-class businessmen, small farmers, and artisans. They disliked monopoly and government interference in the economy. In short, they shared the ideals of their Republican counterparts but rejected the radical measures that seemed to threaten liberty.[14]

This division resulted in a sincere protest, compounded with fear, bitterness, and longing for the prewar status quo. The government's course seemed designed to save the nation, in the words of a West Virginia editor, "by destroying in detail, every element of that free government, which constitutes a Republic." Dissenters were certain that "anarchy, demoralization, and finally disruption" of American freedom would result; because, according to jurist John Marshall, without regard for law and the preservation of personal rights "there is no security for permanence in free government." One need only scan a dissenting newspaper to see the gradual divorce from prowar support as each vigorous policy was announced. Feeling alienated from the war effort, dissenters considered battlefield victories to be "simply triumphs of the army," not of the Northern people. The radical war appeared not only destructive of the South, but of the North as well.[15]

Because they continued to see the United States as the best possible chance for the success of liberty, dissenters continued to view the Union cause as their own. As a result, they were torn between the war's basic purpose and its methods. David Hunter Strother, a Virginian who sided with the North, believed as late as April 1863 that the Rebels could have been repatriated if only the government had offered them something more than "subjugation, ruin, and death." That year conservative army officer Charles Wainwright of New York still argued that the conservative policy could have ben successful if given more time. On radical shoulders alone rested responsibility for the "fearful loss of life, destruction of property, and breeding of hatred" that would result from vigorous prosecution of the war. Soldiers who supported the war but not radicalism had to put up with a vigorous prosecution "practically if not theoretically," or they would face the unwarranted charge of being a traitor.[16]

As many people realized, however, supporting the war while criticizing the government's policies often led to that charge. For men who willingly offered their lives, health, and family's future for the Union, such treatment was bitter. "Dear cousin," began George Sheeks, an Indiana soldier, "being in favor of Disunion or Secesh is the furthest from my mind, yet I believe you would call me a 'Coperhead,' and if you did so with the meaning that I am a Disunionist I would consider it a damnable insult and act accordingly[.] So with your neighbors, if you call them Secesh, they ought to mash your clap trap." One of the best defenses these men could use for their opinions was to denounce extremism of *any* kind, linking abolitionists with secessionists and labeling them all as dangerous to the stability of freedom. "Damn secesh & Abolish without end," as Sheeks vehemently put it.[17]

Despite their heartfelt concerns, critics did not believe revolution was the way to reverse radical policies. They sought political change by working within the system. Dissenters elected sizeable numbers of like-minded candidates to several state legislatures in the fall of 1862, including those of New York and Illinois. However, inconsistencies crippled their efforts to counter radicalization of the war effort, and they were never able to agree on united lines of action. They were placed in the self-defeating position of voting for the men and money necessary to carry on a war to preserve the Union they believed in, while criticizing the policies supported by a majority of Unionists.[18]

Dissent was not a regional phenomenon. It appeared in every Northern state, although its true extent is still a matter of some conjecture. From a survey of opinion found in letters and diaries, one scholar concluded that at least one-third of all Pennsylvania Democrats were dissenters in the fall of 1862. Approximately one-half of the state's Democrats, which represented nearly one-fourth of Pennsylvania's electorate, supported a peace convention in the spring of 1864 to arrange a nonmilitary solution to the war. This was not a call for Confederate victory but for an armistice to stop the fighting while a settlement—short of emancipation—could be negotiated. After Union military victories and Lincoln's reelection in the fall of 1864, Democratic antiwar sentiment virtually died out in Pennsylvania. Probably less than ten percent of the state's Democrats still called for a nonmilitary solution to the war, which was about the number who had consistently opposed any military effort to restore the Union.[19]

The vigorous consensus that remained after the divorce of conservatives strongly supported radical policies. In the eyes of vigorous prosecutors, dissenters were a major stimulus to reinforcing faith in the war effort. Critics were identified with Rebels, as prosecutors ignored their sincere conviction and reacted passionately to all dissent. Critics seemed to prove the notion that Southern ideas had infiltrated the North; in turn, this magnified the threat posed by the rebellion. As a result, radical prosecutors became even more convinced that the vigorous policies were needed to bring the war to a swift and decisive close.

Vigorous supporters, such as Iowa surgeon Seneca Thrall, referred to "the rebels, south *and north*." The difference between them was the greater degree of hate expended on dissenters than on Confederates, for the latter at least were manly enough to fight for their beliefs. The critics' dissonant opinions were hard enough to bear at any time, but especially right after a military defeat. It infuriated New York businessman Robert Ogden that dissenters seemed oblivious to the blood already spilled for the Union; they were apparently willing to throw it away "as nothing." Walt Whitman equated election victories over critics with battlefield triumphs over the armed foe; they were "about as great a victory for us as if we had flaxed General Lee himself."[20]

Prowar supporters expected the wide-ranging consensus of the early months to continue into the vigorous phase of the war effort. They decried "merely partisan prejudices" and were amazed that dissenters could not recognize how the conflict transcended antebellum politics. Democrats who saw the war as "only a party contest" could destroy the simple-minded clarity and focused energy that vigorous prosecutors liked about their policies. New York lawyer George Templeton Strong argued that "it is only their factious opposition that keeps the rebellion alive. Were we united, Jefferson Davis himself would be at a parley."[21]

As dissenters attacked the heart and soul of the Northern war effort, no response was too impassioned to be inappropriate. The opposition had "its origins in H—l," as Indianan James Weiler heatedly described a local Copperhead meeting, "and Beebzebub [sic] the chief of Devils, is there[,] Commander-in-Chief of the whole combined mass of human corruption." Soldiers often filled their letters with impassioned diatribes about the Copperheads, promising retribution when they returned home. Although George Turner of the 92nd Ohio Infantry confessed to hearing more "determined Oaths and solemn vows" by his comrades on the Copperheads than on any other subject, he admitted that "the vocabulary of curses is too short and tame to satisfy some men." Ezra Farnsworth felt something like Rip Van Winkle at discovering how divided was the mood of the North when, after two years of army service, he visited his family in New Hampshire in late 1863. Unanimity had vanished and he lost his temper when overhearing healthy men, who should have been in the army, swear they would kill any enrolling officer who tried to force them into service.[22]

Inevitably, belief in a Copperhead conspiracy sprang up. Jane Grey Swisshelm of Minnesota argued that the early consensus had been a false picture of loyalty. The Democrats had only pretended support so as to get their leaders into high places in government and the military. Not until the time was right, when the administration needed the full support of the nation more than ever, did they make plain their real design—to break up the Union.[23]

The passionate response to dissent was summed up in the flood of letters received by Isaac Funk after he openly denounced Copperheads in the Illinois state legislature. Speaking immediately after a majority of dissenters had been elected to the assembly, Funk employed pure emotion, not ideas, to attack antiwar sentiment. The speech was widely reprinted, and Funk received letters from soldiers and civilians as far away as New York. The correspondents displayed a remarkable sense of relief and pent-up frustration, as if the speech had pricked a bubble of anger, hate, and bitterness. "I thank God in behalf of my bleeding Country," wrote Latitia Moody, "for sending you here to tell the vile Traitors *[sic]* here in the North what all true union Men think of them." Another correspondent particularly liked the fact that Funk was a farmer, which showed the country that it did not have to rely on professional politicians. A farmer "may not be able . . . to spread his ideas over a ten acre lot: or to talk half a day with nothing in the world to say, but . . . what is in his soul he can let out; and let out effectively."[24]

The vigorous response to dissent was a source of bewildered pain to critics of the war. Only seventeen years old when the war began, Alexander Cooper recalled the days of consensus in Camden, Delaware. "The real question . . . was the integrity and preservation of the Union, and we talked about it and discussed it without personal bitterness of feeling." But when the radical policies were adopted, lines were quickly formed between Republicans and Democrats of all ages —from adults to young playmates. The label of Copperhead became a talisman of hate and a license for vigorous prosecutors to act without restraint. Only four years old when Sumter fell, Horace Brown recalled a Copperhead in New Bedford, Massachusetts, who was hated by the grown-ups and therefore became the object of the youngsters' practical jokes. Children had little understanding of the ideological issues of the war; but, with the zeal only ignorant youth could display, "did the best we could to make his life a burden."[25]

Prowar supporters met dissent with blunt action. Across the North they broke up Copperhead meetings, destroyed opposition presses, and held prowar meetings in the same towns where peace meetings had just concluded. They also set up national organizations to distribute propaganda. The most important was the Union League, which organized agencies on the state and local levels. Furloughed soldiers fought Copperheads with their fists and helped to destroy antiadministration presses. In states where dissent was strong, the Republican party relied on fusion politics, calling itself the Union party to strengthen its viability.[26]

The effort to counter dissent was strong and widespread, but the North was far from a closed society during the Civil War. The administration did not uniformly suppress Copperhead newspapers, allowing antiwar voices to be heard if the political consequences of each case justified it. Despite the intense social pressure, dissenters were heard in nearly every Northern town. The intensity of their voices varied according to the competence, energy, or tolerance of local army officials and private citizens. Vigorous prosecutors noted that dissenting charges of despotism were refuted by the fact that critics could make that charge at all and get away with it.[27]

Yet the most devastating argument against dissent was the fact, noted by Northerners at all levels of power, that the Confederates did not want to be conciliated. Even at the height of Copperhead agitation, the enemy never expressed a willingness to reenter the Union if slavery would be safeguarded. The lesson was clear: "Unless we are prepared to acquiesce in all the demands of our enemies, we have no alternative but a vigorous prosecution of the war."[28]

The presidential election of 1864 brought dissent to a crisis. While Democratic prospects had seemed good in the summer of that year, military victories in the fall killed all hopes for the opposition. The Democrats probably would have lost anyway, for the party was wracked with internal problems. Its candidate, George McClellan, had long been perceived as a paragon of conservative policy. Contrary to the party's platform, he pledged himself to a continuation of the war effort. Members of the prowar group, such as Wisconsin soldier James Newton, saw the election as "the most effectual campaign of the war." Those who initially favored McClellan decided to vote for Lincoln when they learned the Rebels liked the Democratic candidate. Soldiers saw the election as involving a clear-cut issue between peace and war. Lincoln's victory put an end to Copperheadism.[29]

Although defeated and consigned to ignominy, dissenters were correct in viewing the radical policies as threats to liberty. Henry Winter Davis of Maryland touched on the key when he warned a Brooklyn audience in November 1861 that self-control was the fundamental issue involved in the war's prosecution. To step outside the legal structure and enact special policies was to "admit the law of necessity to control the law of the land, and leave a discretion which is despotism to provide for the emergencies of the moment." Davis later accepted many points raised by the vigorous prosecution, such as the need to destroy slavery and the Southern aristocracy. But he warned fellow Northerners of the dangers of prosecuting the war through unlawful measures. When citizens could "no longer be masters over themselves, when they can not stop in a moment of passion to reflect upon the limits they themselves have placed around their passions for their own good, and reverently bow before the holy laws, they can no longer be the peaceful, orderly, progressive, and powerful republic of Washington." [30]

Continued faith in their ability to remain "masters over themselves" supported the adoption of vigorous policies. This same faith averted fears of a military despotism, as well as a host of other war-related threats to liberty. Northern defenders of the crusade against slaveocracy knew self-control was a powerful tool in adopting whatever policies were needed to win the war. They also realized that it was possible to drop certain liberties for the duration because they were enlightened enough as a people to restore them at war's end. Their government was a people's government and was not likely to enslave itself. In their view, Northern society was able to conduct a radical war in an oddly conservative manner.

This faith depended on the sometimes subtle shifts in attitude between Republicans and Democrats. The notion that values relating to liberty were of transcendent importance was generally accepted in America. That was one reason why the early consensus of the war was possible, for everyone in the North could agree on its basic purpose. But with the institution of radical policies, Democrats began to perceive the Lincoln administration as subverting those values for partisan purposes—including an illegal abolition of slavery. Democrats began to question the war effort because they saw universal truths—such as the individual's right to own property, to not volunteer for military service, and to be tried in civil court for antiwar dissent—mockingly abused by passion-drive extremists. Those principles had to be respected or passion would destroy them. Republicans and other prowar supporters felt that if republican values were truly transcendent, they *could not* be destroyed by an act of man. The only danger was to the individual's liberty. A temporary loss of personal freedoms was not likely to become permanent. The Northerner who remained faithful to these principles could willingly give them up for the duration, knowing the sound judgment of his fellow citizens would lead to their restoration when victory was achieved. Faith in self-control was a significant difference between prosecutors and dissenters.

Yet, this faith in self-control did not keep vigorous prosecutors from supporting Draconian measures to suppress dissent. If one believed in the concept of self-control and also knew that human beings were a mixture of good and evil tendencies, there was no inconsistency in striving for self-control while believing that one's enemies had lost their virtue. Northerners of all persuasions eventually believed that the South had lost its self-possession. Vigorous prosecutors simply extended that view to include antiwar critics. If dissenters had forgotten the need for self-control, they deserved to be treated as harshly as the Confederates.

The attitude of vigorous prosecutors to constitutionalism illustrated this point. The Constitution loomed as a Colossus of Rhodes for war apologists, demanding some kind of tribute from any American who dared attempt a large, government-sponsored project such as a radical war to save the Union. Ralph Waldo Emerson was certain foreigners could not understand American obsession with the Constitution. "Broad grounds, as, if one party fights for freedom, or for slavery, they can appreciate," he wrote in an 1862 journal entry. "But our constitutionality . . . of one party fighting at the same time . . . *for* slavery in the loyal states, &, in the rebel states, *against* it, is too technical for distant observers."[31]

What Emerson was referring to in 1862 was the use of the Constitution to justify radical policies. While the charter protected all Americans from arbitrary confiscation of property, whether of inanimate or human nature, many vigorous prosecutors believed the Confederates rejected that protection when they rejected the Union. "The man who repudiates all obligations under the Constitution and laws of the United States," argued Ohio lawyer Rutherford Hayes, "is to be treated as having forfeited those rights which depend solely on the laws and Constitution." The attack on slavery was justified by a legal argument —the breaking of a contract implied by participation in the American system of governance—not on moral grounds. Those outside of America could hardly understand why Lincoln's administration would aim to destroy bondage in the seceded states while tolerating it in the loyal slave states.[32]

Other men preferred to phrase it differently; they believed the Constitution had to be held in abeyance for the duration of the conflict. "If the rebellion has assumed such a magnitude," argued an obscure Kentucky officer, "that the constitution does not imbrace means for its suppression sit the document aside for the time." Orestes Brownson phrased it even more stridently when he wrote that "war has its own laws; and, while it lasts, it overrides all other laws, and, if need be, places the Constitution itself, as far as it would be a barrier to its success, in abeyance." Not all prowar supporters would go as far as Brownson in believing "the safety of the nation is the only law which can control military operations, or determine the measures necessary or proper in the [prosecution] of the war." They were much more concerned with balancing constitutional authority with war needs; in the process they justified public manipulation of the charter to clothe war prosecution with authority.[33]

Vigorous prosecutors stressed the pliable nature of the system. The "best feature of a Republican Government," thought Lydia Maria Child, "is the power to modify it, according to the needs of the people." They distinguished between the spirit of the Constitution, which they vowed to respect, and its letter, which they would not allow to impair a war designed to save the integrity of free government. Lincoln spoke for his countrymen when he explained his shift to the vigorous policies. "I felt that measures, otherwise unconstitutional, might become lawful, by becoming indispensable to the preservation of the Constitution, through the preservation of the nation."[34]

This flexibility justified radical measures and allowed Northerners to retain a positive self-image. Not only Republicans but also some Democrats shared this attitude. Large segments of the Democratic party rejected their colleagues' dissenting views and advocated vigorous prosecution. Richard Busteed, an Irish-born New York City lawyer, harangued the crowd at a Union rally in the fervent summer of 1862. "I *was* a Democrat," he explained, "I *am* a loyal lover of my country, whose free institutions I do not care to outlive. . . . I *will be* what her necessities, the convictions of my intelligence and the dictates of my conscience make me." The idea that constitutional authority was dynamic and that the Northern people were intelligent enough to manipulate it without destroying freedom led to a faith that everything could be made right after the war. "Use every effort possible to destroy this rebellion," soldier Harvey Reid of Wisconsin wrote to his father, "and when the Southern people formally acknowledge their error, and express a desire to resume their old relations—extend to them the right hand of fellowship and commence right where we left off, excepting only the losses and changes which the war has made." The change he referred to was abolition.[35]

The vigorous prosecutor's flexibility offered a sharp contrast to the dissenter's ironclad approach to the Constitution. Ironically, the ideological division of the North had its counterpart in the Confederacy. Dissent, spurred by underlying fears for the preservation of liberty, developed among the Rebels. Southern critics believed the Davis administration had become a military despotism, had promoted the centralization of governmental power at the expense of states' rights, and was curtailing the individual liberties of citizens with a stringent enforcement of the draft, the suspension of the writ of *habeas corpus*, and the appropriation of private property for Confederate army use. A key difference lay in the fact that Northern dissent was channeled into an existing two-party political structure, so that vigorous prosecutors could identify critics with the Democratic party. As a result, it was easier for Lincoln to deal with dissenters than it was for Davis, because he could not use institutional means, such as patronage power, to harm them. The two-party system also allowed the public to identify dissenters by directing their attention to Democrats in general. The lines of division were already partially drawn between vigorous prosecutors and conservatives, and they were partisan lines. Davis, on the other hand, was faced with a rather amorphous body of criticism, which was difficult to deal with.[36]

Although Davis adopted radical policies similar to Lincoln's, he and most Confederates could not bring themselves to accept the most radical policy of all—emancipation. The Confederacy may have represented revolutionary trends compared with prewar Southern culture; but compared with the North's vigorous policies, it fell short of truly radical measures. The Confederacy was unable to match the dynamic, innovative, and strengthening belief in the individual displayed by vigorous prosecutors; and Southerners were unable, until the last weeks of the war, to accept radical alteration of slavery, their most cherished institution. Although the Confederate government went farther than conservatives in the North would have been able to accept, the two were ideologically closer than the Copperheads were to the vigorously prowar Northerners.

What separated the mainstream North from dissenters and from Confederates was emancipation and a belief in man's virtuous capability. The Northern dissenter's call for a return to the "Union as it was" lacked the moral fervor of the vigorous prosecutor's call for the "Union as it ought to be." While critics believed that the national structure during the antebellum era had been the best the nation could have hoped for, it was the belief of vigorous prosecutors that the North had been guilty of complying with the slave power. They wanted to expiate that sin. Critics found it difficult to believe that citizens had the moral capacity to take the law into their own hands, or hold it in abeyance, without destroying that law. On this last point they were, like their Southern neighbors, mired in the world of the founding fathers. Dissenters could not dare to question their pessimistic assumptions about human nature.[37]

Consensus and conflict along ideological lines was a prominent feature of Civil War America. Northerners and Southerners began the conflict united in their opposition to what they believed were despotic, antirepublican forces at work in the neighboring section. As the war continued, this unity split wide open. Dissenters in both North and South viewed their government as despotic in its policies, and a new consensus developed on both sides of the line in favor of war as prosecuted by the Lincoln and Davis administrations. Both dissenters and whole-hearted supporters of the government were united by a belief in fundamental republican values of self-government, individual autonomy, and self-control. They differed in their conceptions of who should rule, how much individual autonomy was safe, and how far to trust a citizen's power over self. Those differences, small as they may seem compared to the almost overwhelming unity of belief in basic values, nevertheless guided the course of the conflict from Fort Sumter through the division of war support to the end of the conflict.

Except for a revised attitude toward the revolutionary generation, the only major change in popular ideology to come from the war related to black freedom. While the conservative view did not change, radical war prosecutors slowly began to make room in their consciousness for this hitherto unacceptable idea. Yet the war represented only the beginning of acceptance; the process was not complete until after the war ended and radical reconstruction began.

A turnaround on attitudes toward abolition was greatly aided by the soldiers. Their experience in the field, the bloody battles, long campaigns, and knowledge that slavery was the foundation of the Confederacy worked in favor of growing emancipation sentiment. "There is a mighty revolution a going on in the minds of men on the niger [sic] question," exulted John Russell of Illinois. "It was very galling to some of us that could see the tendency of things but it is useless to move faster than Public opinion can be carried along." Even soldiers who were antiabolitonist before the war eventually supported emancipation. Jasper Barney assured his brother, who was a newly mustered soldier, that he had shared his antiemancipationist views before joining the service but now knew better. "It is my opinion that yourself and the greater part of your Regiment will be in favor of it before you are in the service six months." Army service pushed soldiers farther toward emancipation because it offered them first-hand proof of the degradation, immorality, and suffering caused by the institution. Henry Martyn Cross of New York talked with a black man in Virginia who sadly related how his brother and mother had been sold away long before. "This little incident increased my hatred for the institution," Cross wrote his parents, "for it showed me its cruelty in a stronger light than I had ever seen it in books." [38]

Soldiers and civilians alike recognized that the war was itself the greatest agent of change and that the suffering and reverses borne in it by the Northern people were the key to forging new opinions about black freedom. Charles Francis Adams, Jr., correctly observed that First Bull Run tended "more and more to throw the war into the hands of the radicals, and if it lasts a year, it will be a war of abolition." Other soldiers recognized that the pressures of war in the South would weaken the institution, even if the Confederacy should somehow be victorious. Soldiers saw bondsmen run away every day and knew that slavery was crumbling through the Rebel's fingers, even though abolition had not yet been established as an official war aim of the Union. The only advantage given by the Proclamation, according to John Russell, was "to give systems to emancipation and preserve order" in the process of aiding its internal destruction.[39]

Yet against this stimulus to a radicalized view of the war effort, there worked a counter-influence. Many Northerners as well as Southerners perceived prewar abolitionism as a threat to the established order. A stigma was attached to the term that was strong among soldiers and civilians alike during the conflict. It was ironic, noted George Templeton Strong, that a word denoting commitment to freedom should be considered so threatening in a land of liberty. "I never call myself an Abolitionist," he confessed in his diary, "without a feeling that I am saying something rather reckless and audacious." Many soldiers continued to fear the abolitionist's narrow focus on black freedom as a *sine qua non* of the war effort, believing he was ready to see free institutions destroyed rather than give up his goal. This kind of ultraearnestness spoiled the idea of emancipation in some minds. Commenting on the apparent lack of abolition sentiment among occupation troops at Hilton Head, South Carolina, Charles Francis Adams believed the "ultras in their eagerness have spoilt all."[40]

Another influence working against the growth of emancipation sentiment was widespread racism. Much of that, it seems, stemmed from the notion that black slavery was at the heart of the sectional troubles. Feeling frustrated, angry, and bitter because the black people, by their existence as slaves, had brought on the troubles that tore the soldier from his home and made the nation a bloody, disputed land, the soldier often latched onto the most prominent feature of the slave and blamed the nation's woes on him and his color. These feelings gave rise to racist sentiments, which were expressed in the commonly used phrase "eternal nigger," which often arose like a lamentation from the throats of Northerners.

Soldiers and civilians were careful to distinguish between abolitionism and their new-found commitment to black freedom. They referred to "abolitionism" and "emancipationism," pointing out that the latter was an attitude toward the institution induced only by the slaveholder's attempt to destroy the nation. The distinction was drawn between the "political" abolition of prewar days and the "practical" emancipation advocated by Northerners during the war. Anyone who supported the war for any reason was a practical emancipationist because slavery was an inherent part of the Confederacy. After asserting that blacks were never intended to be slaves, Mary J. Anderson of Kentucky quickly added: "I am no *abolitionist*. I am for closing this war as quick as possible and if [it] can be done by freeing all the niggers let them go."[41]

The great weight of commitment to the Union neutralized the abolitionist stigma and changed popular opinion on slavery. The linking of the slaveholders to the rebellion and the delay in coercing a return of the seceded states set the stage for adoption of emancipation. From September 1862 until early 1863, when the Emancipation Proclamation became effective, favorable opinion continued to grow. Lydia Maria Child observed in late December 1862 that it was becoming much easier to find publishers for antislavery writings. The stigma of abolitionism and long-ingrained acceptance of slavery in America worked against emancipationist sentiment, slowing but not stopping it.[42]

In the army the majority were in favor of freedom for blacks. The opinion ranged from the true prewar abolitionist sentiment to a grudging acceptance of black freedom as a war necessity. Many soldiers would have preferred the Union restored without abolition, but realized this was impossible. The reaction of one officer to an abortive and unauthorized emancipation proclamation by John C. Fremont in Missouri illustrated how some soldiers initially reacted with their emotions to the idea of black freedom. He complained and threatened to resign, but upon "more deliberation, like a sensible man," realized the Union was more important than was the traditional respect for the right to own slaves. John Burrill, a Democrat who was indifferent to the issue of slavery but supported emancipation, illustrated how easily a soldier could reconcile his previous attitude with present necessity. "I regulate my mind to what I think the country needs," he informed his parents. Indeed, some soldiers believed that four-fifths of the army supported emancipation by early 1863.[43]

The arming of freemen also received widespread support among the soldiers. Benjamin Stevens of Iowa continued to prefer his "country as it once was than as it now is" in regard to slavery. Yet he supported the use of black soldiers because the Rebels feared them "more than they would fear Indians. They say their doom has come and nothing but death and destruction awaits them." Faced with the dangers of the battlefield, soldiers were most easily won over to the use of black troops as a way to help ease the burden of fighting the war. As a Vermont artilleryman admitted in his earthy language, "If a bob-tail dog can stick a bayonet on his tail, and back up against a rebel and kill him, I will take the dog and sleep with him—and if a nigger will do the same, I'll do the same by him. I'll sleep with any thing that will kill a rebel."

These men, of course, were not altruistic in their support of black freedom; neither were most other vigorous prosecutors. Emancipation was primarily a war tool; support for black freedom was based on what the citizenry believed could be gotten out of it. As refugees flocked to the armies, soldiers used them as servants, cooks, teamsters, and in a variety of other noncombat capacities, relieving white men of much dreary labor. "What soldier *wouldn't* be an abolitionist under such circumstances," wondered Illinois officer James Connolly.[44]

The growth of a practical attitude toward abolition did not make civil libertarians of Northerners when they considered black rights. What occurred in the crucible of war was nothing more than the first rather small but important step in popular opinion regarding the black condition in America. Because emancipation was primarily a tool of prosecuting the conflict, few Northerners bothered to look beyond to a postwar world of black freemen. John Murray Forbes, an intelligent and politically committed man, spoke for most Northerners who bothered to ponder this question when he expressed his willingness "to trust to the negro's getting his rights, if we can only establish a true democracy; for the greater involves the lesser." The Union had to be restored, he believed, before any serious thought could be given to the freed black problem.[45]

Jacob Behm of the 18th Illinois Infantry probably spoke for those who gave little or no thought to the postwar condition of blacks. A fervent supporter of emancipation, Behm viewed it not only as a vigorous tool in the destruction of the Confederacy but also as a final solution to the evil influence slavery had exerted on national politics for decades. "I hope," he wrote home, "that amond [sic] the results of this war the Negro Question will be banished forever [from] the arena of partie [sic] politics." It is easy to see that Behm was naive to suppose blacks would somehow disappear politically. But before we condemn him, we must realize how largely the rebellion loomed as *the* problem facing America during the war years, tending to blot out consideration of other problems. Vigorous war prosecutors, whose consciousness of the Confederate threat was intensified anyway, were willing to hold the implications of black freedom in abeyance for the duration of the conflict. Tired and frustrated with the constant antebellum agitation over slavery and the resulting civil war, they fervently hoped the conflict would settle this horrible problem once and for all.[46]

Yet among these people there occurred at least the beginning of an awareness that slaves were not inanimate objects of sectional politics. Even among those who consistently favored abolition, few accepted the notion of racial equality or of the average black person's capacity for overcoming the educational, economic, and intellectual disadvantages of two hundred years of bondage. The black person was indeed an object of the war—but importantly, a human object. Northerners who had not bothered themselves with questions of Negro rights before 1861 were now forced to consider them. When the salve was property, it was easy to advocate separation from the master by confiscation. When slaves were freed and gathered like the children of Moses around army camps, it was not easy to ignore their humanity.

Soldiers with progressive views, such as Henry Martyn Cross, boiled the question down to: "Is he a man, or is he not?" Cross rejected racial equality and racial mixing, yet he answered: "We all judge that he is." Only if it was right to "make merchandize [sic] of my body and soul'" would it also be just to do the same to the black person. Soldiers of less progressive views often came to the same conclusion, yet phrased it differently. Nine out of ten soldiers, Frederick Pettit of Pennsylvania believed, considered the Negro to have "rights as a dog has rights," which should be respected. It was Pettit's way of saying that even the lowliest of human creatures deserved some respect. Using dogs as a metaphor for degraded humanity does not bespeak much of a commitment to racial progress, but it indicated a spirit that a large majority of Northern supporters of the war could agree upon. It was a beginning.[47]

CHAPTER 6

Continuity and Change

The war's successful close reinforced the values of liberty in the North as no other event did. It insured that continuity would be the theme of popular ideology throughout the mid-nineteenth century: continuity of rhetoric, of belief, and of self-image. The Civil War generations had clung to the idea of liberty as they knew it during the conflict; after Appomattox, they employed volumes of words to celebrate both the idea and their dedication to it. For them, the war for the Union had become the apotheosis of freedom. Yet even as they celebrated, they recognized that within postwar economics and culture there would also be threats to liberty. Eventually, the Civil War generations came to realize that these developments, which were natural outgrowths of their ideology, were working to change their society.

With the exception of attitudes toward black freedom and the Revolutionary fathers, Northerners were remarkably consistent in their postwar attitudes toward the issues of the conflict. They continued to believe that human bondage had colored all aspects of Southern society. Former General William Averell reminded the readers of his memoirs that a people "derives its character from the character of the labor that supports it,—that free labor created democracy in the North and slave labor the aristocracy of the South." The American union had consisted of two cultures before the war—the free North coexisting with a despotic South ruled by an oligarchy of slaveholders. Freedom was destroyed, or at least nullified, in the lower section by this oligar-chy, which not only ruled politically before the war but also controlled the Confederate army during the conflict.[1]

Because Northerners believed a conflict of cultures had led to the rebellion, they also viewed the war as inevitable. Ignoring their senti-ments of compromise and indecision before Sumter, they now were convinced that North and South had always been antagonistic. Slavery and liberty could not exist in the same nation indefinitely. Southern leaders had alienated the common people from sympathy with the Northern people and the Federal government and the leaders had become jealous of the upper section's prosperity. Thus, the rebellion was "in reality a war of principles irreconcilable," according to Meth-odist clergyman George Corey, "of ideas eternally antagonistic; of civilizations diverse which can never be harmonized." It was a conflict of ideas, with the North fighting against not only the institution of slavery but against human degradation and "an overvaluation of exter-nal possessions in comparison with internal qualities." Veteran Stuart Taylor spoke for many when he asserted that the war had not been fought for plunder or conquest but for the liberty of Northern as well as Southern people. The elimination of slavery benefited the South as much as the North. This belief made the pain of battlefield loss, even after the war, more acceptable. Recalling the Union soldier, Ohio veteran and novelist Albion Tourgee wrote: "Their devotion was not tainted by the flavor of self. They died for the rights of man, for the perpetuity of a government founded on liberty, in deadly conflict with a republic based on the principle of slavery."[2]

Redemption of the despotic South became a prominent theme in postwar commentary. With slavery gone, middle- and lower-class whites could freely engage in the economic and political world. Veterans spoke of a balancing of interests between North and South as the "New Republic" in the lower section took advantage of the great boon offered it by Union victory. The result of the war represented a political revolution for the South, which was essential for the industrial revolution many veterans predicted. They wrote panygerics on the future Dixie, which they believed was "emulating the industrial spirit of the North." According to Gates Thruston, a former officer who spoke before the Society of the Army of the Cumberland in 1890, a "silent, steady wave of emigration and capital is flowing southward. Industries heretofore unknown are unlocking the forces of nature and developing a new wealth." Veterans were certain that as the South adopted the same values that the North had fought for in the war, material prosperity and political rejuvenation were inevitable.[3]

Northerners were confident that the future held better times for everyone because they had believed all along that the heart and soul of liberty-loving America, those who owned small businesses and the working classes, had been denied opportunities by the slavocracy. With slavery eliminated, they asserted that the common people of the South would be able to duplicate the progressive attitudes and prosperous economy of the North. Naively ignoring the power of internalized racial and class prejudice, they pointed to the North as a model of opportunity. Northerners assured themselves and their recent foes that their section, which was grounded on the middle classes, could never aspire to dominate the South. "We are seeking to embody in public economy more liberty, with higher justice and virtue, than have been organized before," C. A. Boutelle of Maine told fellow veterans. "By the necessity of our doctrines we are put in sympathy with the masses of men of all nations. It is not our business to subdue nations, but to augment the power of the common people."[4]

The common people represented the best hope for sectional reconciliation because they held the same interests throughout the world. If common Southerners could be convinced that the war had been beneficial because it eliminated the oligarchy and that adopting the Northern social, political, and economic model would be in their own best interest, the South would truly have been redeemed.

Northerners continued to picture their own common people as the bedrock of the Union. They were the heart not only of the nation but of the war effort as well. Although true leaders were at the head of the government, the people were the mainspring of action. The "popular heart" dictated that the North should attempt to subdue the rebellion, supported the military effort in good and particularly in bad times, and supplied the money, blood, and spirit for the war's successful conclusion. "It is the greatest example in history," thundered Henry Winter Davis on the first Independence Day of the postwar era, "of a great people . . . selecting its own instruments to accomplish the popular will. It was a great movement of the whole mass of the nation."[5]

Even as they celebrated the middle class, Northerners also admitted that they had acquiesced in the dominance of the slavocracy before 1861. The policy of sectional compromise had been designed to preserve the nation and to maintain the domestic peace believed necessary for prosperity. Northern response to the attack on Sumter, however, was the key to averting any threat to their self-image posed by the previous compromise on slavery. Sumter shook Northerners out of their complacency regarding the safety of free institutions. The attack was a vivid reminder of the fragile nature of liberty and the need for a vigilant people to safeguard it. The decision to fight and to sustain the war proved that Northerners were just such a people. George Corey knew that Sumter had "awakened us from our stupor, interrupted our private pursuits and cupidities seriously enough to call us to duty and lead to sacrifice . . . of property and private plans, of ease and comfort, for the cause of the national weal." The conflict had redeemed the North.[6]

The war was a great learning experience for the nation's citizens. Henry Ward Beecher, speaking at the flag raising over Sumter on April 14, 1865, put it succinctly: "We *believed* in our institutions and principles before, but now we *know* their power." The response to Sumter proved the viability of free government and the virtue of the Northern people. Rutherford Hayes believed it "taught ourselves and the rest of mankind, that faith in the fitness of the people to govern." If the people were of correct character, republics were just as capable of subduing internal dissension as were authoritarian states. Individual liberty did not necessarily lead to national disintegration; an individualistic people was not doomed to have a weak governmental power.[7]

Because the conflict focused attention as never before on the authority of the central government, it raised public awareness of the need for a strong, resilient federal power. The lesson was incorporated into nearly all state constitutions written from 1861 through 1912, which included clauses admitting the primacy of the federal government over state governments. As the Stars and Stripes were raised over Sumter immediately after the war, Henry Ward Beecher called it "the flag of sovereignty. The nation, not the States, is sovereign. Restored to authority, this flag commands, not supplicates."[8]

True to their wartime attitudes, Northerners continued to stress the ideological nature of the conflict. They wanted the public to be assured that, as Ohioan Nixon Stewart put it, "behind a war of musketry was a war of mind. Each bullet and each bayonet was guided by a thought." Northerners again stressed the viability of free government, seeing proof that ideological consensus could unite individualistic people in a common cause, focus their energy on a central purpose, and give them the motivation and strength to endure. The war "revealed that the nation has an ideal character," according to George Corey, "a representative value; that its glory springs not from vast extent, populousness, power of wealth, but from the unquestioned dominion of ideas."[9]

Veterans particularly stressed the ideological motives of the war as justification for the sacrifice of life and health. A contest for freedom was morally right and represented common goals that many supported not only during the war but also after the conflict had ended. R. L. Ashhurst, a Pennsylvania volunteer, admitted that Crane's *Red Badge of Courage* was an accurate picture of battle but complained with heartfelt vigor about the novel's lack of ideology. Borrowing from Shakespeare, Ashhurst noted that without ideas pictured as motives, the Northern soldier's work in the war was "but as a tale told by an idiot—full of sound and fury, signifying nothing." If the sacrifice were to be viewed positively and if liberty were truly to be secured in America, Buren Sherman of Iowa believed everyone would have to place the ideology of the conflict in sharp relief and cease being "careless regarding permanency of correct ideas."[10]

The easiest way to forget the ideology was to thoughtlessly embrace sectional reconciliation. Veterans feared that the reasons for the war would be smothered by well intentioned but unwise emotion in the forgive-and-forget postwar atmosphere. "Magnanimity to a fallen foe may be extended to individuals to the full limit of chivalrous generosity," Vermonter W. G. Veazey argued, "but not to the sacrifice of principles." They did not want their work in the conflict to be short changed. As former Sergeant Lucius Bigelow put it, there was bravery in dying for an erroneous cause, as the Rebels did, but "magnificent moral sense" in dying for truth. More importantly, forgetting the goals would lead to negation of the war's result. "We shall not reap the fruits of victory," warned Henry Ward Beecher, "if we suffer these things to be forgotten."[11]

Northerners also displayed their consistency by believing in the nation's military system. Some veterans admitted that the volunteer army had been inefficient and had probably prolonged the war, but they continued to support it. A professional, standing army was still viewed as dangerous to liberty. Moreover, the Northern volunteers proved that reliance on a citizen army was not misplaced. Indisputably, a volunteer army did the job without endangering freedom. After the conflict, the soldiers were easily assimilated back into civilian life.[12]

Impelled by their war experience to more highly regard uniformed service, veterans urged that the military system be improved. The veterans wanted to blend the best of the volunteers—with their republican spirit—with the best of the regulars—with their professional training and experience. They sought to duplicate the voluntaristic spirit of the war, when a citizen soldier adhered to discipline without losing allegiance to civil authority. The proposed changes were like those advocated by Tecumseh Steece during the war—that was, to improve the military awareness of civilians liable to be called on for service. The recommendations included: the introduction of drill exercises and realistic descriptions of battle in the public schools and establishment of a department of military studies in each state university. A national board could select the departments' finest students for admittance to graduate study at military academies before they returned to civilian life.[13]

Veterans retained their faith in the spirit of voluntarism, either ignoring its deficiencies or arguing that defects could be eliminated if only the military system were made even more free in nature. They resembled their Revolutionary ancestors in their continued faith in the spirit that had characterized the early stages of their respective war efforts. The use of conscription and the fact that a proportionately small group of dedicated soldiers carried the weight of each war effort while thousands of less scrupulous and less patriotic men reaped bounties and profits were realities of the war effort that the veterans chose to ignore. Americans after the Revolution and Northerners after Appomattox wanted to believe that a patriotic, republican spirit and a self-denying attitude had impelled them to endure and win; to dwell on the negativity of the war was to deny positive images of self and nation.[14]

The veteran's experience instilled in him an obligation to serve the nation out of uniform as well. "A true citizen," former Ohio officer I. P. Powell said, was really "a soldier awaiting only an adequate cause to be a citizen in uniform." Veterans saw a close relationship between their military and civilian lives. They had learned to be alert and vigilant in the army and carried those traits home. "No citizen soldier of a republic has a right to plead that he has completed his public duty," W. G. Veazey told a group of former Vermont officers. "Our duties as soldiers, we confidently hope, are ended; our duties as citizens may have just begun." [15]

The war experience taught Northerners to perceive little difference between military service and civil responsibility. Indeed, military service had become a hallmark of "right" character; the willingness to offer life, health, and property as a possible sacrifice to the common good had become a test of dedication to liberty. "If ever that unhappy day shall come, when her people shall want the manhood to be such soldiers," predicted veteran William Vilas before his peers, "in that day our republic must fall." I. P. Powell realized that reliance on a professional military to meet all national emergencies meant "the nation has so degenerated that it is no longer capable of self-government." [16]

The theme of continuity was never stronger than in the belief that the war, despite all the threats it contained, had not altered free institutions or values in America. Armed conflict was always dangerous to popular liberty, thought Northerners, but their society had met the challenge splendidly. Even after the conflict, the influence acquired by military leaders, the burden of war debt, and the growth of individual wealth from war industries could still threaten freedom. Yet Northerners seemed to have controlled those threats as well. Even though they had elected several generals to the presidency, witnessed new war-related fortunes amassed by individuals, and were saddled with a huge public debt, they celebrated the stability of free institutions. [17]

Perhaps the most prominent concern for continuity lay in the chance that Northern character would be altered by the harsh experience of war. Predictions were widespread during the conflict that, as former Indiana General Walter Gresham put it, "men familiarized with danger, and accustomed to the discipline of the camp, were to be dreaded by the people, and that a turbulent and indolent soldiery would never again patiently submit to the restraint of law." Yet Northerners were still confident that the dire predictions would prove to be unjustified. Any soldier who left the army morally impure must not have been an honorable man before entering, thought Charles Woodruff. Most often the "discipline of battle purified them," by teaching soldiers "humanity and self-reliance." The bonds forged by common danger led to friendships that ennobled the men. Individual satisfaction was suppressed in favor of common goals, which was a virtue difficult to achieve in civil life. R. L. Ashhurst could not help but believe that the war had purged "from the body of the people, as through fire, the gross elements of egoism, self-seeking, and corruption." The result was an improved sense of morality.[18]

After Appomattox, just as they had during the war, Northerners reached a point of tension in thinking of individualism and the common good. Although they professed to believe the war experience had stimulated allegiance to the common good, they could not give up celebrating individualism and citing it as a prime cause of Northern victory. Northern citizens were products of institutions and ideological values that stressed independence. The citizen's ability to subsume that trait in the common need was further evidence of intelligence and self-control. It was a somewhat delicate yet tenacious balance between individualism and commonwealth that was a characteristic feature of mid-nineteenth-century America.[19]

Northerners could not give up their wartime faith in the radical policies that had helped win the conflict. Some even cited emancipation as the greatest benefit to come from the war, for it settled the sectional division that had troubled America for decades. Only in the context of war could abolition have been accomplished. In peacetime, a consensus in favor of emancipation could not have been achieved due to constitutional questions. Veterans admitted that it was fortunate the Union cause had suffered severe reverses early in the conflict, else the nation might have been restored with slavery intact. Inevitably, another—probably bloodier—war would have developed, which might have led to permanent separation. Veterans celebrated emancipation by referring to "Enlarged Freedom" or "universal freedom." The extension of liberty to the black man was often referred to indirectly, such as Thomas McKee's assertion that "equality of opportunity was to be enjoyed by all men." These citizens were speaking of the incorporation of Negroes into the promise of America.[20]

But Northerners were not consistent in their wartime attitudes toward emancipation. Before 1865, black freedom received most support because it was widely viewed as a necessary war measure. The conflict had witnessed only the smallest step toward the acceptance of black liberty in Northern minds. With the passage of years and of wartime passion, it became easier to accept this idea; in fact, it even appeared to be a natural outgrowth of the war to save white liberty. As Pennsylvanian Edward Spangler put it, the war "logically ended in the abolition of slavery and the perpetuity of republican institutions." Men like Spangler looked back after the war and for the first time, from the lofty perspective of hindsight, saw the ideological common sense of emancipation.[21]

A protean vision of liberty developed as a result of the full acceptance of black rights. Northerners widely admitted that the founding fathers had erred in avoiding the issue of slavery, but most seemed to understand why they had done so. In 1787 the world had "not agreed as to the measure or extent of the rights of man," according to John Palmer of Illinois. While believing that some had the right to enjoy liberty, the founding fathers were also certain that others had an equal right, due to their fitness for it, to rule. Thus liberty in the eighteenth century was seen as *"partial"* by former General John Logan because it excluded blacks. The fathers had sought to avoid the divisiveness of slavery by cloaking it in a robe of constitutional silence, a worthy enough compromise for 1787, but this was inadequate for more progressive times. Northerners believed they had learned "that freedom is a right inherent in man himself," as poet James Russell Lowell argued, "and not a creature of the law, to be granted to one class of men or withheld from it at the option of another."[22]

The arrival at this enlightened stage of a commitment to black rights was partly due to ruminations on the part of Northerners as the years passed; but there were other factors as well. The failure of Johnson's reconstruction program to neutralize prewar Southern power elites and the onset of congressionally directed radical reconstruction led many Northerners to advocate immediate granting of black civil rights. Ulysses Grant believed that in 1865 most citizens of his section did not favor black suffrage. Those who opposed suffrage thought that Negroes would need a long time to educate themselves to the responsibilities of citizenship. But the apparent failure of presidential reconstruction brought Grant quickly to accept black voting as a counterweight to the political power of Southern conservatives. As Marylander Henry Winter Davis put it, numbers were more important than intelligence and blacks were certainly smart enough to know which Southern politicians were their enemies and which were their friends. Black military service was another impetus. "When it became expedient to put arms into their hands in order that they might fight for the Union," John Logan reasoned, "the necessity of investing them soon or late with the privilege of the ballot became apparent at once." Army service was in some ways a supreme test of devotion for white Northerners, and they could hardly deny that it also proved the black soldier's devotion to freedom.[23]

Increased awareness of liberty's nature contributed to what Northerners felt was their greater sensitivity to black problems. "The voice of war summoned us back to our original ideal," George Corey told a meeting of the Grand Army of the Republic. Northerners felt the need to square that ideal with the social facts of American life. "Liberty is the first fact," continued Corey, "liberty resting not upon a distinction of race, a claim of territory or hereditary privileges, not even upon political traditions or compacts of any sort, but directly upon the primal rights of man." This represented a strident hope for the setting aside of racism in dealing with black problems by recognizing *all* people's right to enjoy freedom. As Rutherford Hayes put it just after leaving the presidency, the North's increased awareness of personal responsibility for the "conduct and character of the nation" led to a "disposition to deal conscientiously and humanely with all the weaker races in our midst."[24]

Lest we overestimate Northern enthusiasm for black rights, consider the commentary of former Colonel Stanley Matthews in 1874. He assured an audience of veterans that Negroes had been given the suffrage and "equal participation in all strictly civil and political rights." A series of constitutional amendments had raised blacks to the level of whites in civil privileges, but that was as far as Northerners were willing to go. "We have done our whole duty when we have established and enforced, in favor of the freedmen, *equality of right under the law*. The rest, whatever it may prove to be, he must do for himself. We confer upon him his personal freedom, his civil rights, his political liberty. His social position must be the result of social forces, with which Government, neither State nor National, has any right to interfere." That was all Northerners had asked for white men in nineteenth-century America, and it was all they were willing to give blacks.[25]

Thus, the citizenry of the North were certain they had fulfilled their republican duties toward the Negro. This, and the saving of the Union, were stupendous enough for comparison with their hallowed ancestors. The war had been nothing less than "the *experimentum crucis* of free government." Many derived great satisfaction in placing themselves on the same level of intelligence, virtue, and dedication as Washington, Jefferson, and Patrick Henry. Civil War generations sought to make certain they would be judged as equals to the founding fathers, not only by their own calculations but by their descendants' as well. Augustus Buell, a former Yankee artilleryman, dreamed of the day his progeny would "pride themselves on our deeds as we now pride ourselves on the deeds of our Revolutionary grandshires."[26]

Many Northerners believed that they had gone beyond the example of their ancestors, particularly in granting black freedom. The seeds of this attitude had been sown when they realized that the compromise on slavery in 1787 had led directly to war in 1861. The Revolutionary generations might have been able to envision a perfect governmental system, but they were not able to implement it. The war had unsettled a blind acceptance of the infallibility of the founding fathers and made Northerners realize their ancestors had acted with faulty judgment. "It is preposterous to suppose," wrote Grant, "that the people of one generation can lay down the best and only rules of government for all who are to come after them."[27]

The war taught Northerners that history itself was not sacrosanct. They knew from battle experience that great historical outcomes often depended on "purely fortuitous circumstances," and how "chance or the bias of the historian" dictated to succeeding generations who should receive the credit for the victories. E. B. Parsons had believed before the war that "everything written as history must be literally true and beyond question," especially if it related to the Revolution. The innumerable controversies that attended nearly every major battle of the Civil War, along with conflicting written records, taught Parsons not to implicitly trust the historian's work. He began to apply that lesson to the Revolution as well.[28]

Thus there appeared many comparisons of the participants of America's two great wars. Commentators pointed to the different percentages of men mobilized for military service, the number of enemy ships captured or destroyed, the number of Loyalists in colonial America, and the horrible difficulties of maintaining an efficient Continental army, often ignoring the same evidence in their own war. Aside from this kind of questionable analysis, there was the glaring fact that the rebellion represented a deathblow to American nationality as the founding fathers had constructed it. "To save, is a greater achievement than to found a nation," observed Henry Barnum, "to curb the disintegrating forces is more difficult than to energize the experimental powers of liberty."[29] Believing by the nature, magnitude, and results of their war that a superior character had to have sustained it, Northerners began to back away from the hero worship that had characterized their attitudes toward the Revolutionary generation. The Revolution would still hold a nostalgic place in their hearts but would no longer constitute the heroic benchmark against which all subsequent events in American history would be judged insignificant.

Except for changes in black America and a more mature attitude toward their ancestors, Northerners emerged from the war feeling secure in their ideology. "In no other instance has a conflict such as that of our Civil War so little harmed or even changed the institutions of a country," marveled Nathaniel Southgate Shaler of Kentucky. Because the war settled the single most divisive issue—slavery versus freedom—liberty seemed secure after Appomattox. "Hereafter the strifes of party and our political differences will hardly touch the fundamental principles or even the forms of our institutions," former President Rutherford Hayes argued. Political quarrels would be over "mere questions of administration," not over basic issues at the heart of the American experiment. The war, in short, achieved ideological unity for the nation. Sectional freedom had been hammered into a national faith.[30]

These paens were good for after-dinner speeches at veterans' reunions, but they were hollow and dangerous according to a small group of postwar commentators. Doubters argued that liberty was not consummated by the war or by the reconstruction that followed; they offered a telling critique of the self-image so important to most Northerners.

The most incisive critic was veteran and novelist Albion Tourgee. He strove to demonstrate the inadequacy of the Northern attitude in dealing with race and class, which had always been intimately united in Southern culture. Far from being fulfilled, liberty was a dynamic organism that continually evolved. Embalming liberty for posterity's sake, as the Northern victors tried to after 1865, only stifled its further development. Not much had changed; Northerners still bothered themselves very little after the war with the issue of black rights, abandoning the Negro to white racial and class domination. Tourgee's was a lonely but eloquent voice of protest.

Two of his more significant books on the subject, *An Appeal to Caesar* and *The Veteran and His Pipe*, were published in the mid-1880s, shortly after the failure of radical reconstruction. A skillful writer, Tourgee set the theme effectively in the former work with an introduction detailing a meeting with newly elected President Garfield. Both he and the president expressed deep concern that a golden moment for true reconstruction of Southern society by fostering black equality had been carelessly thrown away. The frustration of having missed a historic opportunity for the nation was mirrored by the pain of Garfield's death only a few months later.[31]

An Appeal to Caesar was a straight forward analysis of the Southern social problem; but it was not as effective as *The Veteran and His Pipe*, a wonderfully ironic book with three fictional characters: a maimed Union soldier, his pipe "Blower," and a former Confederate soldier and present friend of the Yankee, Pascal Raines. The one-armed veteran talks to his pipe, the only surviving companion of his war days, and sets the tone of the book by sketching out his moral dilemma. The nation had grown, its values changing with prosperity, until the moral fervor of the war had been eclipsed by greed. "We are told that the day of sentiment has passed, and the era of practicality begun. . . . Devotion to the rights of man is an innocent weakness; gain the one thing needful." The book is shot through with longing for the heady righteousness of freedom that so captivated the war generations in the sixties; Tourgee's reference to it as "nostalgic" evokes the way his society had lost that fervor.[32]

The strength of Tourgee's critique lay not only in the clarity and force of his writing style but in his long war service, during which he suffered painful injuries, and his reform work later in North Carolina. Tourgee had the insight and courage to admit his naivety. He believed that his thoughts were typical of most soldiers; with slavery gone, in a year or so the South would blossom into a new North. Tourgee was ignorant of how race and class combined to keep Negroes enslaved before 1861 and was utterly naive about the continuance of that combination into reconstruction. He believed that the influence of the Northern economic and social example, along with the influx of Northern capital and migrants, would quickly transform the lower section. Freedom for blacks was no more difficult than granting them the opportunity to vote and hold office. "The fact that a man was free and had the abstract right to enjoy and exercise the privileges of the citizen seemed to be thought all that was necessary to transform a million of unlettered slaves into an equal number of self-governing citizens to whom the power of the ballot might safely be intrusted."[33]

Although understandable, this naivety led to the abandonment of blacks by most Northern citizens after the war. After reconstruction, even radical Republicans washed their hands of the problem. Pascal Raines, the noble Confederate veteran, bitterly denounced the Northern lack of moral fiber. He had admired his blue-coated enemy during the war because of the moral fervor exhibited in their struggle for freedom. Their dedication to principles was a sign of their capacity for self-sacrifice, which, he believed, had been fulfilled after Appomattox. Although Raines had admired Northerners during the war, afterward he came to despise them. The abandonment of the black people held a double meaning for Northern character and for the condition of blacks in the South. It was Northerners' moral responsibility, thought Raines, to aid the people they had wrenched from slavery. As long as the operation of free institutions in the North was not jeopardized, Northerners cared not whether blacks were truly free or whether liberty existed in the South. Through Pascal Raines Tourgee argued that the sectional condition of freedom was still current. "Your sham enfranchisement of the negro has satisfied your vanity and allowed you to make easy terms with that conscience which once underlay your patriotism."[34]

Tourgee tried to bring his fellow citizens back to an awareness of the war's causes and its results. It was right to forget the hatred but not the reasons for that hatred, or the moral rightness of the conflict. Northerners continued to believe in the prewar delusion that the United States was one nation; thus forgetting the real cultural cleavages they had come to recognize during the war. Despite what Northerners believed, the South did not change. The aristocratic and racial themes of Southern culture continued to characterize the postwar world. Believing that Northern institutions had been imposed on Southern society by the war and reconstruction, people felt their job was done. Tourgee knew that there were Northerners, "who having assented to what was done when it *was* done, are now so sure that what they then did was in all respects perfect and complete that they do not deem it worth their while to work out the reckoning anew."[35]

The great falsehood of the North, as Tourgee bitterly expressed it, was in not teaching the Negro how to be a citizen. If the newly emancipated Negro was truly to enjoy opportunity, it was essential that he gain the education necessary to make full use of his suffrage. Tourgee chalked it up to racism in the North, believing his fellows shared the Southern spirit toward the black man in all things except "as to his natural right to be free and to exercise the rights of the freeman." Yet the government's refusal to aid blacks to overcome the horrible economic, social, and educational disadvantages of bondage illustrated the limits of the ideal of freedom as held by most Northerners. Tourgee advocated an educational system, supported and operated by the federal government, to teach not only blacks but poor whites in the South to use their political opportunities to effect social and economic change. By including poor whites, Tourgee showed his awareness that the problem of race in the South was also a problem of class. There existed a long tradition of government interference to break down what was perceived as class privilege, one of the most prominent examples being the battle over the Second Bank of the United States in Andrew Jackson's administration.[36]

But the Southern problem had the complicating factor of race, and Northerners had trouble dealing with it. Built on the assumption of a community of interests, Northern ideology worked when applied to a group of people united by common color, cultural heritage, and aspirations for prosperity. European immigrants, who shared most of these characteristics, either quickly or inevitably adopted the other traits in order to be incorporated into the promise of America. Except for a small and easily controlled population of free blacks, it had never before been necessary for republicans of the North to face the problem of incorporating color into their ideological fold. This was an enormous challenge for Northerners after the war; not surprisingly, they failed.

Tourgee asked his countrymen to make a radical departure. He proposed government activism more akin to the modern liberal state than to government in mid-nineteenth-century America, and that made Tourgee's a strident, but largely ignored, voice. At the heart of his stance was a constantly unfolding, dynamic conception of liberty. As noted before, veterans also expressed adherence to this concept, but they meant it in very simple terms of expanding existing conceptions of liberty to the South. What Tourgee wanted after the conflict was a different paradigm, not expansion of the boundaries of the existing paradigm. Maine veteran Joshua Chamberlain seemed to have briefly touched on the spirit of Tourgee's message without referring to him, admitting that the idea of freedom he and his comrades had during the war was far too "simple." Instead, he now knew liberty was a "very complex thing" when applied to "the people and to all the interests and industries that we have in this country." Chamberlain called for his fellow veterans to expand their consciousness, to break the old mold if need be, for "so long as men and women are down-trodden and have not a fair and equal chance to make the most of themselves; so long freedom is short of its glorious goal."[37]

Tourgee was joined by a small group of protestors, some of them well-known, but none with the power to achieve substantial changes in public attitudes or policy. John Logan, who was a war hero and prominent politician, wrote an imposing tome arguing that the oligar-

chy that had started the war was still intact after the failure of reconstruction. Other critics, such as General Nelson Miles, were much less
overt, slipping veiled protests into their war memoirs. Here and there
men openly cringed at the idea, inadvertently fostered by the cele-
brants of Northern virtue, that *all* Northerners had supported emancipation during the war. There was no room for celebration of Copperheads, and that hurt dedicated Unionists who had opposed or regretfully
endured radical policies. Charles Anderson, a brother of Fort Sumter
hero Robert Anderson, knew people were "naturally prone to reason
out some morally sublime cause for every grand consequence . . . so
we have come to convince ourselves that our noble Union Armies and
'The Whole North' could have had no other motive in that War than
the abolition of slavery."[38]

Disillusionment with popular attitudes about virtue seem to have
been more widespread among the intellectual elite than among any
other group in the Civil War generations. Ralph Waldo Emerson
admitted that his society had not fulfilled the promise for moral rejuvenation offered by the war. Intellectuals who had been soldiers also
came to the same conclusion. They blamed the breakdown of virtue
on increased wealth and aggressive individualism, which they saw as
insensitive to civic duty. This belief broke the barrier between themselves and their Southern opponents. Disillusioned veterans began to
feel they had more in common with ex-Confederates than with Northern businessmen because they and the Rebels had both fought for
ideals rather than personal gain in the war.[39]

When non-elite members of the Civil War generations criticized
society, they did not argue that their ideology was a failure. Instead,
they concentrated on the postwar social, political, and economic developments that seemed to threaten what they had fought for. Speaking
to their own generations as well as to succeeding generations, they
gave evidence of a deep concern for the perpetuation of liberty.

Ironically, one of the chief threats to liberty was the progress that
had always been a prominent feature of their national faith. Veterans
were overjoyed at the prosperity of their nation after the war and
celebrated it as a natural fruit of their ideology. Yet they sought to
continue the balance between self and the whole and between prosperity and civic duty. Refusing to believe the economic developments of

the postwar period demanded a different ideology, they firmly expected the self-controlled individual to maintain this delicate balance. Self-interest and morality, according to veteran Lucius Bigelow, were the two operative forces in the world; working together, they accounted for progress. Self-interest impelled the citizen to develop new machines, to exploit resources, and to open new markets. In its healthy moral state, self-interest meant "the high materialities of this life, honestly won, and wisely and virtuously enjoyed." The "diseased exaggeration" of self-interest led to speculation, thievery, and "insane acquisitiveness." Self-interest had to be infused with a healthy moral sense to prevent harm both to the individual's character and to the commonwealth.[40]

The danger of not heeding this lesson was a pleasure-seeking, self-centered society, which was exactly what many members of the Civil War generations feared. They complained of "these times of gain-getting [and] pleasure-seeking," when, according to Ohioan Carl Adae, the "every-day pursuit of gain" was "rendered most keen by the unprecedented competition in every path of business or profession." This "money-making, money-powered people" was a particularly bitter fact for Robert Carter, a veteran of both the volunteer army and the postwar regulars. "Liberty has been converted into license," he complained. Young people seemed "restless and uneasy unless they are being continually saturated with abnormal and unwholesome pleasures, luxuries and unnatural excitement." Immigrants seemed to pose a particular threat because, as former nurse Annie Wittenmyer expressed it, so many of them "care nothing for the American Republic and her free institutions, only as they will add to their physical comfort and personal aggrandizement."[41]

The protean economy threatened traditional cultural values of America, with wealthy businessmen replacing lawyers and politicians as role models and accumulation replacing service as a worthy end. It all implied a strong connection between gain and effort, the former defined primarily as material gain and the latter primarily as business activity. This disgusted Oliver Wendell Holmes, Jr., who ordered his entire memory of his war experience as a contrast to this nexus. A hardheaded, realistic warrior in the 1860s, Holmes knew the soldier did not fight for money and that often he could expect little if any ideological gain from his suffering. The nature of combat all too often prevented the individual from feeling that his personal effort had any benefit in prosecuting the war, yet Holmes and thousands of men like him continued to serve. This was the blind faith of the soldier that Holmes has become so justly famous for describing. It was a rejection of commensurate profit for work and a glorification of the vital element of the chase as opposed to the reward. If a man could march across a muddy field, watching the minie balls plopping beside his feet, and continue to believe in the value of staying in line, he touched the vital spirit of living and striving that several lifetimes spent in dark counting rooms could not equal. For Holmes, the battle experience was a refutation of the values of a cash economy and a reaffirmation of self-sacrifice.[42]

Veterans feared that the dynamic progress of the economy would destroy the traditional values of the simple culture in which they were raised. Concentration of wealth in individual and corporate hands could seduce the possessors into forgetting the common good. Henry Ward Beecher pointed out that his society went to great lengths to limit a man's political power yet placed no limit on his accumulation of wealth, which was just as powerful a tool for evil as was political strength. The corporations greatly aided individual accumulation by promoting the material wealth of a small group of investors over the small businessman. Veteran John Logan feared the rise of class dissension as a result of this form of businessman's oligarchy, especially when corporations exercised undue influence over local and state governments.[43]

The aggregation of wealth, whether in the hands of an individual or a group of individuals, was bound to be deterimental to the many. "With increase of wealth usually come self-indulgence, pride, and extravagance," argued former Illinois General Augustus Chetlain. "All history shows that wealth grows more and more ambitious, and that poverty in the same ratio becomes more restless and discontented." The indulgence of the rich and the restlessness of the poor were double perils to the solid middle class, which was the bulwark of the nation. The growth of business organizations from the regional, family-owned scale to national, publicly owned corporations represented a trend toward centralized power in the hands of a few that seemed to threaten individualism among the middle ranks of society, turning the self-employed into the other-employed. "The small manufacturer has almost disappeared," Albion Tourgee wrote. "The small dealer has been absorbed. The small manufacturer has become a foreman; the small merchant an agent." It was a trend toward control of opportunity for the many by the few.[44]

Machine government in the cities was just as serious a threat to the individual. The accumulation of local political power, with its adjuncts of vote-buying, nepotism, and graft, had the same debilitating effect on virtue as the accumulation of financial power among businessmen. For Albion Tourgee, this lessening of individual opportunity called for federal intervention in the economy and in local politics.[45]

Yet, government intervention was not as clear-cut a solution as Tourgee suggested. His conception of federal responsibility outstripped that of most Americans of his time. Bishop Ireland stated the dilemma felt by most when he admitted that corporations were potentially dangerous threats to liberty, but to destroy them would be equally dangerous. American ideology legitimated the individual's right to prosper, and Northerners of the late nineteenth century saw that right utilized to the full in the careers of many businessmen. To suppress the rise of the corporations as they had suppressed the rebellion would be an artificial answer, thought Ireland, since it did not take into account the natural inclination of the individual to prosper on the strength of his own endeavors. Ireland's answer was to proselytize among the businessmen, to "preach unceasingly the doctrine of justice and charity."[46]

It is easy to assume that Tourgee would have laughed at the good bishop's solution, but Ireland did explain the almost tragic paradox of Northern ideology in the face of large-scale progress. To arrest the development of business organization was implicitly to deny key elements of that ideology, including the right to exploit the economic environment for personal gain. The gray area lay in figuring out how and where to curb power without denying opportunity to businessmen. If the answer to this question did not eliminate unfair accumulation of power and wealth, it suggested the ideology was inadequate. Deciding where and when the businessman forgot his duty to balance personal and communal good and how to correct that imbalance,

without destroying the ideology that led to the problem, proved difficult.

Unable to go beyond the tenets of their ideology, for that would be
an admission of its inadequacy, Northerners tried to admonish people
to be better citizens. They reemphasized public virtue as a necessary
foundation for good government and encouraged fellow citizens not to
become complacent in the celebration of their victory in the war.
Walter Gresham argued that the existence of graft, demagoguery, and
corruption in national politics did not necessarily mean Northern values had been destroyed. Just as the North had temporarily lost hold of
virtue by acquiescing to the slave power before Sumter and then
purged itself by going to war to redeem that error, so would the solid
mass of virtuous citizens reawaken and fight the corruption. "The
honest and industrious elements of society are patient and long-suffer-
ing," Gresham said, "they have an almost instinctive sense of the
approach of real danger, and when the crisis comes, they will surely
assert themselves as they did in 1861."[47]

Their religious adherence made the Civil War generations hypersen-
sitive about the apparent demise of their values. They read postbellum
cultural changes as fatal threats to the ideology that had nurtured them
before the war and which they had defended on the fields of Antietam
and Chickamauga. The central and ominous theme for them was a too-
strident sense of individualism and a degradation of self-control. R. L.
Ashhurst spoke in 1896 of "that undue development of the individual
which is one of the vices of modern life," while another veteran from
Massachusetts referred to "man, his welfare and ambitions, taking
precedence over that of the Republic." Thus, the notion that government had an obligation to protect individual welfare seemed to over-
ride the citizen's sense of obligation to protect his government.[48]

These critics referred to a weakening of self-control, which meant a
loss of responsibility for balancing what was good for the individual
with the common good. The belief in civic duty was weakened, and
self-indulgence and self-development assumed greater and greater significance. This change in values was a logical result of individualism.
The kind of aggressive, accumulative individualism they saw developing in America had little to do with control of passion, with commonwealth, or even with a producer-oriented society. It did have a lot to

do with the modern, consumer-oriented society of today. The change took succeeding generations farther away from a sense of what the Civil War had meant to the American character. The war generations were in the unenviable position of seeing, before their eyes, their children and grandchildren growing apart culturally as they grew older.

This was not the usual lack of understanding of a younger generation for an older, which exists in all time periods. But the immediate postwar generations, those coming of age in the 1880s and particularly the 1890s, represented a watershed in cultural change. This was the time when America became a modern nation, when the economic organizations assumed nation-wide focus, and when the basis for subsequent large-scale economic progress was firmly laid. This new generation had much less in common with the men and women who fought the Civil War than those born in the 1820s through the 1840s had had with their fathers.[49]

Veterans understood this change all too keenly. William Averell wrote of "the living wall of another generation," whose lives "respond to a different environment from that which surrounded Americans before the war." The mere passage of time and the fact that subsequent generations did not have personal experience of the Civil War were obstacles to an awareness of what had been at stake in the conflict. But added to that was the great peace and prosperity of the postwar world, which lacked centrally divisive issues such as slavery and despotism. "In this day of wonderful prosperity," mused Alfred Andreas, formerly of the 12th Illinois Infantry, "when the differences between political parties is so slight . . . when self-interest, the accumulation of wealth, the desire for prominence, the quest of fashion and luxury, have full sway over the whole civilized world," it was difficult for the new generation to understand that a very different political and economic climate had existed before Sumter. "To-day our children ask us why we went voluntarily into that awful war," continued Andreas, "and we cannot give what is to them a satisfactory answer."[50]

For the generations born after the Civil War, acquisitiveness gradually appeared to be a brighter beacon. Frugality and industry as the proper roads to advancement were not necessarily dismissed; after all, the adult was to a large degree the product of his childhood training.

But newer values began to assume prominence as well. The individual will to succeed, rather than self-disciplinary virtues, began to be seen as the avenue of success. The stress was on personal qualities rather than on moral virtues. The ideal of community service became for many a rationale for commercialism, as service lost much of its connotation of disinterestedness and assumed a greater share of profit motive. For succeeding generations, "an overriding emphasis on the pursuit and use of wealth" became prominent. As a result, the businessman's role was increasingly separated from his social responsibilities. Individualism began to assume its modern definition of a self more or less separated from the whole. The "lonely crowd" waited just around the corner.[51]

The development of a consumer-oriented segment of the economy also aided in the breakdown of self-control as a prominent cultural value. It was the precursor to today's highly sophisticated consumer marketing and consumption patterns, a market geared toward offering a variety of consumer products to as wide an audience of buyers as possible. The consumer-oriented economy began to assume significance in the last two decades of the century and quickly developed more sophisticated means of producing and distributing a bewildering variety of products. Installment buying, mail-order catalogues, extensive advertising, cheap prices, and a nationwide focus were made possible by volume production and marketing. The consumer industry reached its maturity in the 1920s and continued to develop until, in the mid-twentieth century, it reached an unprecedented stage of cultural influence.[52]

Although in its infancy after the Civil War, the consumer economy began to affect attitudes toward self and others. The immediate gratification of the desire for possession was a powerful force that countered the value of self-denial. The language used by students of consumer culture vividly revealed this point. Using phrases such as "new freedom from self-denial and from repression," they highlighted the threat to self-control that was inherent in a consumer-oriented economy. The development of this culture confirmed the shift from producer to consumer values in society, from an active thrust toward building to a passive receptivity that did not become fully dominant until the mid-twentieth century. Advertising, in the words of historian David Pot-

ter, was "geared to the stimulation or even the exploitation of materi-
alistic drives and emulative anxieties and then to the validation, the
sanctioning, and the standardization of these drives and anxieties as
accepted criteria of social value."[53]

In short, the Civil War generations spoke more of their fears than of
the actual demise of virtue in their lifetime. The shift in cultural values
was slow, but their estimate of its result was not inaccurate. Their
ideology had long been adaptive to changing social and economic
conditions. It was flexible enough to accommodate the existence of
Southern slavery; it was resilient enough to handle the threat posed by
the rebellion, the attack on Fort Sumter, the suffering caused by the
war, the creation of a huge army with its potential for militarism, and
the adoption of radical policies. Why did the ideology not adapt to and
survive modernization?

All the threats related to the sectional struggle were external to the
ideology. Slavery and rebellion originated outside the boundaries of
this ideology, at least as far as Civil War Northerners were concerned.
They grew up with sectional liberty and the existence of Southern
bondage. Sumter and the war were delivered to them by hot-headed
Southerners. War and the radical policies were the result of forces
other than virtue; indeed, they were the results of nonvirtuous acts.
Thus, while all of these external forces proved to be threats to republicanism, none of them were fatal because no inconsistencies arose and
no unexplainable questions resulted from the clash of Northern values
and outside forces.

Modernization, however, was an internal threat, supported by the
very definition of the ideology. Progress and prosperity were keynotes
of both the process of modernization and the ideology. The difference
was one of scale. Although the members of the Civil War generations
supported progress, many had trouble with the tremendous technolog-
ical and organizational advances of the late nineteenth century. Progress had assumed such a guise as to baffle and worry them. Antebellum
Northerners firmly believed that their society was a prosperous one.
But by mid-twentieth-century standards, it was still an economy of
scarcity. Their expectations were correspondingly scaled down. Illinois soldier Byron Carr spoke for many when writing to his father
from war-torn Missouri in 1862. "I never cared for more than enough

to keep me from want when I am unable to earn my living," he reflected. "It is true I would like to have enough to make my children comfortable but if I can leave them the same inheritance I have received from you, an ability & willingness to provide for themselves by the labor of their own hands and an honest independence which scorns the bread of idleness I shall consider that they are rich & will be satisfied."[54]

Carr offered a testament to the producer values of his culture, expressing typical willingness to do physical labor for his living and affirming realistic expectations of life in an economy that was more noted for its future potential than for its material opulence. Born in 1832, Carr expressed sentiments appropriate to a culture that viewed progress as tempered with virtue. When modernization burst the bounds of their ideological expectations and left the balance of self and the commonwealth spinning in its wake, the Civil War generations realized how much the world had changed.

Civil War veterans were alarmed when they began to witness unexpectedly rapid and long-ranging progress. They were troubled; for they believed in progress but were fearful of its cultural effects. They found themselves replaced by a younger generation that seemed less dedicated to the values they had fought to preserve and that lived according to new ideas that were more conducive to greater opportunity in the new America. As the era of the war for the Union passed into history, the nation left behind many of the values the war generations had fought for. Before 1861, Northerners had always been impressed by what the Revolutionary fathers had wrought. Mingled with the celebration of their own accomplishment, there were now doubts about what they themselves had wrought. Faith in the preservation of liberty remained strong, but progress had never before appeared to be so easily divorced from virtue.

Notes

Introduction

1. Robert Penn Warren, *The Legacy of the Civil War: Meditations on the Centennial* (New York: Random House, 1961), 64, 69, 76.

1. Freedom and Self-Government

1. *Cincinnati Daily Commercial*, May 6, 1861, in *Northern Editorials on Secession*, ed. Howard Cecil Perkins, vol. 2 (New York: D. Appleton, 1942), 826–27.

2. Alexis de Tocqueville, *Democracy in America*, vol. 1 (1835; reprint, New York: Alfred A. Knopf, 1980), 64–65.

3. Albion W. Tourgee, *Murvale Eastman, Christian Socialist* (New York: Fords, Howard and Hulbert, 1890), i; M. D. Leggett address, *Report of the Proceedings of the Society of the Army of the Tennessee at the Sixth Annual Meeting, Held at Madison, Wisconsin, July 3rd and 4th, 1872* (Cincinnati: Society of the Army of the Tennessee, 1877), 38.

4. George Sidney Camp, *Democracy* (New York: Harper and Brothers, 1841), 134–38, 225–27.

5. *Ibid.*, 88–89.

6. J. R. Pole, *The Pursuit of Equality in American History* (Berkeley: University of California Press, 1978), 1, 3, 35; Gordon S. Wood, "The Democratization of Mind in the American Revolution," *Leadership in the American Revolution: Papers Presented at the Third Symposium, May 9 and 10, 1974* (Washington, D.C.: Library of Congress, 1974), 64, 71–72, 76, 78–83.

7. Message to Congress in Special Session, July 4, 1861, *The Collected Works of Abraham Lincoln*, vol. 4, ed. Roy P. Basler (New Brunswick, N.J.: Rutgers University Press, 1953), 438.

8. John A. Logan, *The Great Conspiracy: Its Origin and History* (New York: A. R. Hart,

1886), 668; George Bancroft, "The Office of the People in Art, Government, and Religion," in *Literary and Historical Miscellanies* (New York: Harper and Brothers, 1855), 423–24; Andrew Carnegie, *Triumphant Democracy* (New York: Charles Scribners Sons, 1886), 348, 451; George Bancroft, "Self-Government: Address of Welcome to the American Historical Association," *Papers of the American Historical Association*, vol. 2, no. 1 (New York: G. P. Putnam's Sons, 1888), 11.

9. Robert E. Shalhope, "Toward a Republican Synthesis: The Emergence of an Understanding of Republicanism in American Historiography," *William and Mary Quarterly* 29, no. 1 (January 1972): 51–59; Bernard Bailyn, *The Ideological Origins of the American Revolution* (Cambridge, Mass.: Harvard University Press, 1967), 35, 53, 55–59; Gordon S. Wood, *The Creation of the American Republic, 1776–1787* (Chapel Hill: University of North Carolina Press, 1969), 23.

10. Shalhope, "Toward a Republican Synthesis," 50–55, 70; Wood, *Creation of the American Republic*, 66–69, 93, 413–25; Drew R. McCoy, *The Elusive Republic: Political Economy in Jeffersonian America* (New York: W. W. Norton, 1980), 67–70; Gordon S. Wood, *Creation of the American Republic*, 415, 608, 610.

11. Joyce Appleby, *Capitalism and a New Social Order: The Republican Vision of the 1790s* (New York: New York University Press, 1984), 14–23, 66, 79, 84, 86–101; Lance Banning, "Jeffersonian Ideology Revisited: Liberal and Classical Ideas in the New American Republic," *William and Mary Quarterly* 43, no. 1 (January 1986): 3–19; Joyce Appleby, "Republicanism in Old and New Contexts," *William and Mary Quarterly* 43, no. 1 (January 1986): 20–34.

12. Drew R. McCoy, *The Elusive Republic*, 67–70.

13. John A. Logan, *The Volunteer Soldier of America* (Chicago: R. S. Peale, 1887), 376–78.

14. Despite its widespread appearance in the commentary of nineteenth-century Americans, the concept of self-control has not been fully explored by historians. It is often assumed, for instance by John Diggins and others, to have mainly religious roots. Gerald Linderman notes how self-control was intimately tied up with concepts of manliness. I argue for its close relationship to a sense of civic responsibility. Obviously, these and many other arguments are partially right, for the concept of self-control was loosely defined and used by nineteenth-century Americans. That, however, does not lessen its validity as an organizing tool in understanding culture. John P. Diggins, *The Lost Soul of American Politics: Virtue, Self-Interest, and the Foundations of Liberalism* (New York: Basic Books, 1984), 98; Gerald F. Linderman, *Embattled Courage: The Experience of Combat in the American Civil War* (New York: Free Press, 1987), 28–31.

15. George Bancroft, "The Progress of Mankind," in *Literary and Historical Miscellanies* (New York: Harper and Brothers, 1855), 485–86.

16. Alexis de Tocqueville, *Democracy in America*, vol. 2, 121–22; ibid., vol. 1, 243.

17. George Sidney Camp, *Democracy*, 100, 102–4.

18. Alexis de Tocqueville, *Democracy in America*, vol. 2, 142; Gardner Brewer to Mrs. Alexander, December 6, 1864, Atwood Papers, Illinois State Historical Library; Joseph P. Thompson, *Revolution Against Free Government Not a Right But a Crime* (New York: C. A. Alvord, 1864), 39–40.

19. [Nahum Capen], *The Republic of the United States*, v; M. D. Leggett address, *Report of Proceedings, Society of the Army of the Tennessee, Sixth Meeting*, 1872, 38.

20. Alexis de Tocqueville, *Democracy in America*, vol. 1, 418; Jean H. Baker, *Affairs of Party: The Political Culture of Northern Democrats in the Mid-Nineteenth Century* (Ithaca,

N.Y.: Cornell University Press, 1983), 71–107; Ruth Miller Elson, *Guardians of Tradition: American Schoolbooks of the Nineteenth Century* (Lincoln: University of Nebraska Press, 1964), Chap. 10, 213, 217–18; Carl E. Kaestle, *Pillars of the Republic: Common Schools and American Society, 1780–1860* (New York: Hill and Wang, 1983), 79–103; Bernard Wishy, *The Child and the Republic: The Dawn of Modern American Child Nurture* (Philadelphia: University of Pennsylvania Press, 1968), 47–48; Sam Pickering, "A Boy's Own War," *New England Quarterly* 48, no. 3 (September 1975): 362–77.

21. J. Edward Leithead, "The Revolutionary War in Dime Novels," *American Book Collector* 19, nos. 8–9 (April–May 1969): 15; Peter Karsten, *Patriot-Heroes in England and America: Political Symbolism and Changing Values Over Three Centuries* (Madison: University of Wisconsin Press, 1978), 83–89; William Alfred Bryan, *George Washington in American Literature, 1775–1865* (New York: Columbia University Press, 1952), 18–21, 74–83.

22. B. M. Palmer, *A Discourse Before the General Assembly of South Carolina, on December 10, 1863* (Columbia, S.C.: Charles P. Pelham, 1864), 10; Stephen Elliott, *"New Wine Not to be Put into Old Bottles"* (Savannah, Ga.: John M. Cooper, 1862), 10; William Wilkins Glenn journal, January 1, 1864, *Between North and South: A Maryland Journalist Views the Civil War*, ed. Bayley Ellen Marks and Mark Norton Schatz (Rutherford, N.J.: Fairleigh Dickinson University Press, 1976), 115.

23. Stephen Elliott, *"New Wine Not to be Put into Old bottles,"* 14–15.

24. B. M. Palmer, *A Discourse Before the General Assembly of South Carolina*, 11; Charles C. Jones, Jr., to C. C. Jones, January 28, 1861, *The Children of Pride*, ed. Robert Manson Meyers (abridged ed., New Haven, Conn.: Yale University Press, 1984), 43; John M. Morehead to Thomas Ruffin, November 23, 1861, *The Papers of Thomas Ruffin*, vol. 3, ed. J. G. DeRoulhac Hamilton (Raleigh, N.C.: Edwards and Broughton, 1920), 195.

25. Steven Hahn, "The Yeomanry of the Nonplantation South: Upper Piedmont Georgia, 1850–1860," in *Class, Conflict, and Consensus: Antebellum Southern Community Studies*, eds. Orville Vernon Burton and Robert C. McMath, Jr. (Westport, Conn.: Greenwood Press, 1982), 48; F. N. Boney, *Southerners All* (Macon, Ga.: Mercer University Press, 1984), 1–5; Stephen Elliott, *"New Wine Not to be Put into Old Bottles,"* 12.

26. James Oakes, *The Ruling Race: A History of American Slaveholders* (New York: Alfred A. Knopf, 1982), xii–xiii, 34, 39–41, 127, 192–97.

27. Andrew Jackson Donelson, quoted in William Barney, *The Road to Secession: A New Perspective on the Old South* (New York: Praeger, 1972), 51; B. M. Palmer, *A Discourse Before the General Assembly of South Carolina*, 11.

28. David Hubbard, quoted in J. Mills Thornton, III, *Politics and Power in a Slave Society: Alabama, 1800–1860* (Baton Rouge: Louisiana State University Press, 1978), 213.

29. "Cornerstone Speech," March 21, 1861, quoted in Henry Cleveland, *Alexander H. Stephens, In Public and Private* (Philadelphia: National, 1866), 717–29; Address at Sanitary Fair, April 18, 1864, in *The Collected Works of Abraham Lincoln*, vol. 7, ed. Roy P. Basler (New Brunswick, N.J.: Rutgers University Press, 1953), 301–2.

2. The Nation's Crisis

1. Oliver Wendell Holmes, Sr., "Bread and the Newspaper," *The Complete Writings of Oliver Wendell Holmes*, vol. 8 (Boston: Houghton Mifflin, 1899), 13; Oliver Wendell Holmes, Sr., "The Wormwood Cordial of History: With a Fable," *Atlantic Monthly* 8 (October 1861): 511.

2. Eric Foner, *Free Soil, Free Labor, Free Men: The Ideology of the Republican Party Before the Civil War* (New York: Oxford University Press, 1970), 87–98; David Brion Davis, *The Slave Power Conspiracy and the Paranoid Style* (Baton Rouge: Louisiana State University Press, 1969), 19–23.

3. Seneca B. Thrall to wife, June 6, 1863, "An Iowa Doctor in Blue: The Letters of Seneca B. Thrall, 1862–1864," ed. Mildred Throne, *Iowa Journal of History* 58, no. 2 (April 1960): 155; Elizabeth Blair Lee to Samuel Phillips Lee, January 31, 1861, " 'On the Qui Vive for the Long Letter': Washington Letters from a Navy Wife, 1861," ed. Virginia Jeans Laas, *Civil War History* 29, no. 1 (March 1983): 46; *Chicago Daily Journal,* April 17, 1861, in *Northern Editorials on Secession,* vol. 2, ed. Howard Cecil Perkins (New York: D. Appleton, 1942), 808.

4. Edward A. Acton to wife, July 11, 1862, " 'Dear Mollie': Letters of Captain Edward A. Acton to His Wife, 1862," ed. Mary Acton Hammond, *Pennsylvania Magazine of History and Biography* 89, no. 1 (January 1965): 36.

5. Nathan B. Webb diary, June 26, 1862, Illinois State Historical Library; Maria Lydig Daly diary, December 31, 1861, *Diary of a Union Lady, 1861–1865,* ed. Harold Earl Hammond (New York: Funk and Wagnalls, 1962), 81; speech, August 1862, Leonard Swett Papers, Illinois State Historical Library. Swett was a U.S. congressman from Illinois.

6. J. W. Price to uncle, March 27, 1862, Robert J. Price Papers, Indiana Historical Society; John Stahl Peterson, "The Issues of the War," *Continental Monthly* 5 (1864): 276; entry in 1862 journal, *The Journals and Miscellaneous Notebooks of Ralph Waldo Emerson,* vol. 15, ed. Linda Allardt (Cambridge, Mass.: Harvard University Press, 1982), 205.

7. Walt Whitman, *The Eighteenth Presidency!,* ed. Edward F. Grier (Lawrence: University of Kansas Press, 1956), 32; W. H. Price to "Sir," May 2, 1864, Price Papers, Illinois State Historical Library; Moses G. Atwood to Moody Kent, February 10, 1861, Atwood Papers, Illinois State Historical Library.

8. Henry M. Alden, "Pericles and President Lincoln," *Atlantic Monthly* 11 (March 1863): 388; Captain Caldwell to brother, January 11, 1863, Caldwell Family Papers, *Civil War Times Illustrated* Collection, U.S. Army Military History Institute.

9. Entry of March 20, 1861, *Diary of George Templeton Strong: The Civil War, 1860–1865,* eds. Allan Nevins and Milton Halsey Thomas (New York: Macmillan, 1952), 113; undated essay, Ramson Bedell Papers, Illinois State Historical Library.

10. Julius Power to Mattie, July 14, 1861, Jacob B. and Julius Power Papers, Indiana Historical Society; Lydia Maria Child to Sarah Shaw, June 14, 1861, *Lydia Maria Child: Selected Letters, 1817–1880,* eds. Milton Meltzer and Patricia G. Holland (Amherst: University of Massachusetts Press, 1982), 386; entry in 1863 journal, *Emerson Journals and Notebooks,* vol. 15, 350.

11. Diary entries, January 4, 27, 1861, *Diary & Letters of Rutherford Birchard Hayes,* vol. 2, ed. Charles Richard Williams (Columbus: Ohio State Archaelogical and Historical Society, 1922), 2, 4.

12. Kenneth M. Stampp, "Lincoln and the Secession Crisis," *The Imperilled Union: Essays on the Background of the Civil War* (New York: Oxford University Press, 1980), 163–88; Jacob D. Cox, "War Preparations to the North," in *Battles and Leaders of the Civil War,* vol. 1, eds. Robert Underwood Johnson and Clarence Clough Buel (New York: Thomas Yoseloff, 1956), 85.

13. Francis Wayland, Jr., "No Failure for the North," *Atlantic Monthly* 11 (April 1863): 502.

14. George Sidney Camp, *Democracy* (New York: Harper and Brothers, 1841), 100.

15. Walt Whitman, *The Eighteenth Presidency!*, 37; Andrew Johnson speech, February 26, 1863, *The Papers of Andrew Johnson: Volume 6, 1862–1864*, eds. Leroy P. Graf and Ralph W. Haskins (Knoxville: University of Tennessee Press, 1983), 149; John Lothrop Motley to wife, June 23, 1861, *The Correspondence*, vol. 2 (New York: Harper and Brothers, 1900), 150.

16. Phillip S. Paludan, "The American Civil War Considered as a Crisis in Law and Order," *American Historical Review* 77, no. 4 (October 1972): 1019, 1021–25, 1027, 1030.

17. David E. Beem to wife, July 27, 1862, Beem Papers, Indiana Historical Society; Andrew B. Jackson, "The Panic at Washington After the Firing on Fort Sumter," *Wisconsin Magazine of History* 3, no. 2 (December 1919): 244.

18. Entry of April 30, 1861, "The Civil War Diaries of Anna M. Ferris," ed. Harold B. Hancock, *Delaware History* 9, no. 3 (April 1961): 230; Samuel James Reader to father, January 13, 1861, "The Letters of Samuel James Reader, 1861–1863," *Kansas Historical Quarterly* 9, no. 1 (February 1940): 27; Reader to Frank Reader, March 25, 1861, ibid., 28; Reader to Frank Reader, May 12, 1861, ibid., 30; Levi Adolphus Ross diary, July 1, 1863, Illinois State Historical Library; Jane Grey Swisshelm to *St. Cloud Democrat*, April 11, 1863, in *Crusader and Feminist: Letters of Jane Grey Swisshelm, 1858–1865*, ed. Arthur J. Larsen (St. Paul: Minnesota Historical Society, 1934), 211; John Stahl Peterson, "The Issues of the War," 275.

19. Entry of April 25, 1861, *Diary of George Templeton Strong: The Civil War*, 135; Charles Eliot Norton to A. H. Clough, May 27, 1861, *Letters of Charles Eliot Norton*, vol. 1 (Boston: Houghton Mifflin, 1913), 234.

20. *Boston Post*, April 16, 1861, in *Northern Editorials on Secession*, vol. 2, 740; Lydia Maria Child to Sarah Shaw, June 14, 1861, *Child: Selected Letters*, 385; *Cincinnati Daily Commercial*, May 6, 1861, in *Northern Editorials on Secession*, vol. 2, 828.

21. Message to Congress in Special Session, July 4, 1861, *The Collected Works of Abraham Lincoln*, vol. 4, ed. Roy P. Basler (New Brunswick, N.J.: Rutgers University Press, 1953), 439.

22. Lemuel Adams autobiography, 47, Illinois State Historical Library; Lydia Maria Child to William Lloyd Garrison Haskins, April 30, 1863, *Child: Selected Letters*, 427–28.

23. William Camm to John Moses, January 24, 1863, "Diary of Colonel William Camm, 1861–1865," *Journal of the Illinois State Historical Society* 18, no. 4 (January 1926): 936; R. Delavan Mussey to Joseph Barratt, July 26, 1861, Mussey Papers, Joseph Regenstein Library, University of Chicago; James A. Connolly to Mary, July 21, 1863, *Three Years in the Army of the Cumberland: The Letters and Diary of James A. Connolly*, ed. Paul M. Angle (Bloomington: Indiana University Press, 1959), 106.

24. Jane Stuart Woolsey to friend, May 10, 1861, *Letters of a Family During the War for the Union, 1861–1865*, vol. 1, eds. Georgeanna Woolsey Bacon and Eliza Woolsey Howland (New Haven, Conn.: Tuttle, Morehouse, and Taylor, 1899), 67, 70–71.

25. Paul C. Nagel, *One Nation Indivisible: The Union in American Thought, 1776–1861* (New York: Oxford University Press, 1964), 13, 21–23, 104, 259, 281.

26. Ulysses S. Grant, *Personal Memoirs*, vol. 2 (New York: Charles L. Webster, 1885), 542; Henry Winter Davis speech, July 4, 1865, *Speeches and Addresses* (New York: Harper and Brothers, 1867), 574; Albion W. Tourgee, *An Appeal to Caesar* (New York: Fords, Howard, and Hulbert, 1884), 25–26.

27. *Bangor Daily Evening Times*, May 4, 1861, in *Northern Editorials on Secession*, vol. 2, 758; John Lothrop Motley to wife, July 14, 1861, *The Correspondence*, vol. 2, 177.

28. Daniel John McInerney, "Abolition and Republican Thought: History, Religion, Politics," (Ph.D. diss., Purdue University, 1984), 42–44, 66, 167–72, 275–92.

29. A. Caldwell to brother, March 7, 1863, Caldwell Family Papers, *Civil War Times Illustrated* Collection, U.S. Army Military History Institute.

30. Chauncey H. Cooke to mother, July 28, 1863, "A Badger Boy in Blue: The Letters of Chauncey H. Cooke," *Wisconsin Magazine of History* 4, no. 4 (June 1921): 455; Walter Stone Poor to George Fox, May 15, 1861, "A Yankee Soldier in a New York Regiment," ed. James J. Heslin, *New-York Historical Society Quarterly* 50, no. 2 (April 1966): 115; Theodore Bost to parents, April 27, 1861, *A Frontier Family in Minnesota: Letters of Theodore and Sophie Bost, 1851–1920*, ed. and trans. Ralph H. Bowen (Minneapolis: University of Minnesota Press, 1981), 181.

31. Moncure D. Conway, *The Rejected Stone: Or Insurrection vs. Resurrection in America* (Boston: Walker Wise, 1861), 20; Lydia Maria Child to Lucy Searle, June 5, 1861, *Child: Selected Letters*, 383; Child to Lucy Searle, June 9, 1861, ibid., 384.

32. Moncure D. Conway, *The Rejected Stone*, 8, 78.

3. Coming to Terms

1. James M. McPherson, *Ordeal by Fire: The Civil War and Reconstruction* (New York: Alfred A. Knopf, 1982), 383; entry of May 19, 1861, *A Philadelphia Perspective: The Diary of Sidney George Fisher Covering the Years 1834–1871*, ed. Nicholas B. Wainwright (Philadelphia: Historical Society of Pennsylvania, 1967), 390.

2. Thomas Scott Johnson to "folks," August 25, 1864, "Letters from a Civil War Chaplain," *Journal of Presbyterian History* 46, no. 3 (September 1968): 224; Cornelia Hancock to sister, July 14, 1864, *South After Gettysburg: Letters of Cornelia Hancock from the Army of the Potomac, 1863–1865*, ed. Henrietta Stratton Jaquette (Philadelphia: University of Pennsylvania Press, 1937), 126; Hancock, undated essay, ibid., 5.

3. Abner R. Small, *The Road to Richmond*, ed. Harold Adams Small (Berkeley: University of California Press, 1939), 185.

4. James A. Garfield to Harry, April 14, 1861, *The Wild Life of the Army: Civil War Letters of James A. Garfield*, ed. Frederick D. Williams (East Lansing: Michigan State University Press, 1964), 6; copy of Sullivan Ballou to wife, July 14, 1861, Adin Ballou Papers, Illinois State Historical Library.

5. Dietrich C. Smith to Carrie Pieper, June 24, 1862, Smith Papers, Illinois State Historical Library.

6. Ebenezer Hannaford, "In the Ranks at Stone River," *Harper's New Monthly Magazine* 27 (November 1863): 814.

7. Ebenezer Hannaford, "In Hospital After Stone River," *Harper's New Monthly Magazine* 28 (January 1864): 263–64.

8. Ibid., 264–65.

9. Ruth A. Whittemore to Charles, November 3, 1861, " 'Despotism of Traitors': The Rebellious South Through New York Eyes," ed. Walter Rundell, Jr., *New York History* 45, no. 4 (October 1964): 335; Whittemore to Charles, March 30, 1862, ibid., 340; Whittemore to Charles, June 5, 1862, ibid., 344.

10. Whittemore to Charles, August 10, 1862, ibid., 346; Whittemore to Charles, December 27, 1862, ibid., 349; Whittemore to Charles, May 17, 1863, ibid., 353; Whittemore to Charles, June 19, 1863, ibid., 355.

11. Whittemore to Charles, June 19, 1863, ibid., 355.

12. Entry of December 25, 1861, "The Civil War Diaries of Anna M. Ferris," ed. Harold B. Hancock, *Delaware History* 9, no. 3 (April 1961): 232–33; Ferris diary, March 2, 1862, ibid., 234–35; Ferris diary, December 14, 1862, ibid., 242.

13. Ferris diary, April 3, 1865, ibid., 258.

14. Walt Whitman to Thomas Jefferson Whitman, March 18, 1863, *Walt Whitman: The Correspondence, Volume 1, 1842–1867*, ed. Edwin Haviland Miller (New York: New York University Press, 1961), 80; Whitman to Louisa Van Velsor Whitman, July 7, 1863, ibid., 114; Whitman to Lewis K. Brown, August 15, 1863, ibid., 134.

15. Whitman to Louisa, August 25, 1863, ibid., 137; Whitman to Louisa, March 22, 1864, ibid., 204; Whitman to Louisa, March 29, 1864, ibid., 205.

16. Whitman to Louisa, April 10, 1864, ibid., 209; Whitman to Thomas Jefferson Whitman, May 23, 1864, ibid., 225.

17. Ralph Waldo Emerson, "Public and Private Education," in *Uncollected Lectures by Ralph Waldo Emerson*, ed. Clarence Gohdes (New York: William Edwin Rudge, 1932), 4.

18. Mrs. Furness, "Our Soldiers," *Atlantic Monthly* 13 (March 1864): 364.

19. Montgomery Schuyler Woodruff, "The Civil War Notebook of Montgomery Schuyler Woodruff," ed. Frederick M. Woodruff, *Missouri Historical Society Bulletin* 29, no. 3 (April 1973): 166, 168.

20. Estelle Morrow diary, January 4, 1862, Indiana Historical Society; Morrow diary, April 10, 1862, ibid.; Morrow diary, May 20, 1862, ibid.

21. Henry Henney to sister, April 1, 1863, Henney Papers, *Civil War Times Illustrated* Collection, U.S. Army Military History Institute; Henney diary, April 26, 1863, ibid.; Daniel Holt to wife, May 15, 1863, Holt Papers, New York State Historical Association.

22. J. Spangler Kieffer to Robert Weidensall, October 4, 1862, Robert Weidensall Papers, George Williams College Library.

23. John Russell to sister, April 15, 1862, Russell Papers, *Civil War Times Illustrated* Collection, U.S. Army Military History Institute; William Wheeler to M., November 6, 1862, *Letters of William Wheeler of the Class of 1855* (Cambridge, Mass.: H. O. Houghton, 1875), 364.

24. Edward Dicey, *Six Months in the Federal States*, vol. 2 (London: Macmillan, 1863), 292.

25. H. L. Brush to Charles, January 23, 1863, Brush Family Papers, Illinois State Historical Library; William W. Belknap, "The Obedience and Courage of the Private Soldier," in *War Sketches and Incidents, Iowa Commandery, Military Order of the Loyal Legion of the United States*, vol. 1 (Des Moines, Iowa: P. C. Kenyon, 1893), 164.

26. Jacob Heffelfinger diary, June 27, 1862, *Civil War Times Illustrated* Collection, U.S. Army Military History Institute.

27. John R. Rankin, "What I Thought at Antietam," pp. 1, 8–10, Benjamin Wilson Smith Papers, pt. 2, Indiana Historical Society.

28. Ibid., 9, 12–13.

29. Walter Carter to unidentified, December 24, 1862, *Four Brothers in Blue: Or, Sunshine and Shadows of the War of the Rebellion* (1913; reprint, Austin: University of Texas Press, 1978), 212–13.

30. Charles Eliot Norton, "The Advantages of Defeat," *Atlantic Monthly* 8 (September 1861): 363–64.

31. Undated diary entry, *James Freeman Clarke: Autobiography, Diary and Correspon-*

dence, ed. Edward Everett Hale (1891, reprint, New York: Negro Universities Press, 1968), 286–88.

32. Undated address at funeral of William Lowell Putnam, ibid., 274–75; undated sermon, ibid., 284.

33. Thomas Wentworth Higginson to mother, November 1, 1861, *Letters and Journals of Thomas Wentworth Higginson, 1846–1906*, ed. Mary Thacher Higginson (1921; reprint, New York: Da Capa Press, 1969), 159–60.

34. Lydia Maria Child to Sarah Shaw, July 25, 1863, *Lydia Maria Child: Selected Letters, 1817–1880*, eds. Milton Meltzer and Patricia G. Holland (Amherst: University of Massachusetts Press, 1982), 433; Ralph Waldo Emerson to Benjamin and Susan Morgan Rodman, June 17, 1863, *The Letters of Ralph Waldo Emerson, Volume 5*, ed. Ralph L. Rusk (New York: Columbia University Press, 1939), 332.

35. Mary Christian Percy to Henry, September 24, 1862, Augustus Cowan Papers, Illinois State Historical Library; Leander Stem to Amanda, November 7, 1862, "Stand By the Colors: The Civil War Letters of Leander Stem," ed. John T. Hubbell, *Register of the Kentucky Historical Society* 73, no. 3 (July 1975): 305. The American death rate was a little over two percent per one thousand in the 1850s. In contrast, the town of Deerfield, Massachusetts, lost fourteen percent of its contribution to the Union army, 303 men. If one counted only those soldiers killed on the battlefield, the army's death rate may have approximated the civilian rate, but that was only a small proportion of the total losses caused by the war. See Edward Meeker, "The Improving Health of the United States, 1850–1915," *Explorations in Economic History* 9, no. 4 (Summer 1972): 362; Emily J. Harris, "Sons and Soldiers: Deerfield, Massachusetts, and the Civil War," *Civil War History* 30, no. 2 (June 1984): 170.

36. Speech at Great Sanitary Fair, Philadelphia, June 16, 1864, *The Collected Works of Abraham Lincoln, Volume 7*, ed. Roy P. Basler (New Brunswick, N.J.: Rutgers University Press, 1953), 395.

37. Lewis O. Saum, "Death in the Popular Mind of Pre–Civil War America," *American Quarterly* 26, no. 5 (December 1974): 479–81.

38. W. H. Clune to Maggie, April 16, 1862, Clune Papers, State Historical Society of Iowa, Des Moines; Onley Andrus to Mary, April 26, 1863, *The Civil War Letters of Sergeant Onley Andrus*, ed. Fred Albert Shannon (Urbana: University of Illinois Press, 1947), 53.

39. Walter Carter to unidentified, September 23, 1862, *Four Brothers in Blue*, 129; Frederick L. Hitchcock, *War From the Inside* (Philadelphia: J. B. Lippincott, 1904), 71–72; William Wheeler to L. R. P., January 5, 1864, *Letters*, 439.

40. Samuel Osgood, "The Home and the Flag," *Harper's New Monthly Magazine* 26 (April 1863): 668; Oliver Wendell Holmes, Sr., "My Hunt After 'The Captain'," *Atlantic Monthly* 10 (December 1862): 744.

41. Jim Higginson to Henry, October 9, 1862, quoted in Bliss Perry, *Life and Letters of Henry Lee Higginson* (Boston: Atlantic Monthly, 1921), 174; Estelle Morrow diary, January 8, 1862, Indiana Historical Society; Robert McAllister to family, July 16, 1864, *The Civil War Letters of General Robert McAllister*, ed. James I. Robertson (New Brunswick, N.J.: Rutgers University Press, 1965), 463.

42. Helen Myers to Edward, October 3, 1862, *Vermont General: The Unusual War Experiences of Edward Hastings Ripley, 1862–1865*, ed. Otto Eisenschiml (New York: Devin-Adair, 1960), 47.

43. Ibid., 48. Other Northeners indicated that the loss of acquaintances in the war

simply reaffirmed their commitment to its prosecution. "So many of our own citizens [of Chelsea, Massachusetts] had already fallen, that a feeling of personal responsibility to country rested upon every loyal citizen as it had not done before." Charles A. Currier, "Recollections of Service With the Fortieth Massachusetts Infantry Volunteers," MOLLUS-Massachusetts Commandery Collection, U.S. Army Military History Institute.

44. John T. Trowbridge, "The Field of Gettysburg," *Atlantic Monthly* 16 (November 1865): 618.

45. Edward Tabor Linenthal, *Changing Images of the Warrior Hero in America: A History of Popular Symbolism* (New York: Edwin Mellen, 1982), ix–xvii, 4–5; entry of August 12, 1863, " 'A Monotony Full of Sadness': The Diary of Nadine Turchin, May, 1863– April, 1864," ed. Mary Ellen McElligott, *Journal of the Illinois State Historical Society* 70, no. 1 (February 1977): 58–59.

46. Jane Grey Swisshelm to *St. Cloud Democrat*, August 2, 1863, *Crusader and Feminist: Letters of Jane Grey Swisshelm, 1858–1865*, ed. Arthur J. Larsen (St. Paul: Minnesota Historical Society, 1934), 248–49.

47. Howard Stevens to uncle, July 21, 1863, Harrisburg Civil War Round Table– Gregory Coco Collection, U.S. Army Military History Institute; entry of April 15, 1862, "Diary of Colonel William Camm, 1861 to 1865," *Journal of the Illinois State Historical Society* 18, no. 4 (January 1926): 862.

48. Stephen I. Rogers to father and mother, May 19, 1864, Rogers Papers, Illinois State Historical Library; Rutherford Birchard Hayes to wife, July 30, 1861, *Diary and Letters of Rutherford Birchard Hayes*, vol. 2, ed. Charles Richard Williams (Columbus: Ohio State Archaeological and Historical Society, 1922), 50; entry of March 1, 1863, *Federals on the Frontier: The Diary of Benjamin E. McIntyre, 1862–1864*, ed. Nannie M. Tilley (Austin: University of Texas Press, 1963), 117.

49. Franc B. Wilkie, *Pen and Powder* (Boston: Ticknor, 1888), 248–49. A typical consolation letter is Victor H. Gould's to G. W. Clark family, December 22, 1863, Gould Papers, Illinois State Historical Library.

50. Edward Payson Goodwin to wife, May 12, 1865, Goodwin Papers, Illinois State Historical Library; Edward Dicey, *Six Months in the Federal States*, vol. 2, 292–93.

51. Oliver Wendell Holmes, Sr., "The Inevitable Trial," in *The Complete Writings of Oliver Wendell Holmes*, vol. 8 (Boston: Houghton Mifflin, 1899), 116; Charles Eliot Norton to G. W. Curtis, June 24, 1864, *Letters of Charles Eliot Norton*, vol. 1 (Boston: Houghton Mifflin, 1913), 269.

52. John Stahl Peterson, "The Issues of the War," *Continental Monthly* 5 (1864): 274.

53. Oliver Edwards, "My Recollections of the Civil War," p. 102, Illinois State Historical Library; Lydia Maria Child to Mattie Griffith, December 21, 1862, *Child Letters*, 421–22.

54. Charles Russell Lowell to Josephine Shaw, June 18, 1863, *Life and Letters of Charles Russell Lowell*, ed. Edward W. Emerson (1907; reprint, Port Washington, N.Y.: Kennikat Press, 1971), 260–61; Lowell to Josephine, July 24, 1863, ibid., 280.

55. Charles Eliot Norton to G. W. Curtis, July 26, 1861, *Letters*, vol. 1, 237–38; Norton, "The Advantages of Defeat," 362, 365.

56. Joshua Lawrence Chamberlain, *The Passing of the Armies* (New York: G. P. Putnam's Sons, 1915), 18; William Wilkins Glenn journal, April 14, 1865, in *Between North and South: A Maryland Journalist Views the Civil War*, eds. Bayley Ellen Marks and Mark Norton Schatz (Rutherford, N.J.: Fairleigh Dickinson University Press, 1976), 195.

4. Liberty and War

1. Charles Nordhoff, "Two Weeks at Port Royal," *Harper's New Monthly Magazine* 27 (June 1863): 113.

2. Wilder Dwight to unidentified, July 16, 1861, *Life and Letters of Wilder Dwight* (1867; reprint, Boston: Little, Brown, 1891), 50; Emily Elizabeth Parsons to mother, February 13, 1863, *Memoir of Emily Elizabeth Parsons* (Boston: Little, Brown, 1880), 54; Thomas James Owen to father and friends, December 19, 1863, *"Dear Friends at Home . . .": The Letters and Diary of Thomas James Owen, Fiftieth New York Volunteer Engineer Regiment, During the Civil War*, ed. Dale E. Floyd (Washington, D.C.: U.S. Government Printing Office, 1985), 19.

3. Charles Russell Lowell to Henry L. Higginson, January 21, 1863, *Life and Letters of Charles Russell Lowell*, ed. Edward W. Emerson (1907; reprint, Washington, New York: Kennikat Press, 1971), 232; Lowell to Josephine Shaw, June 17, 1863, ibid., 259.

4. Lowell to Higginson, September 10, 1864, ibid., 340–41; Lowell to Shaw, June 17, 1863, ibid., 259.

5. Entry in 1863 journal, *The Journals and Miscellaneous Notebooks of Ralph Waldo Emerson*, vol. 15, ed. Linda Allardt (Cambridge, Mass.: Harvard University Press, 1982), 379.

6. Samuel Osgood, "The Home and the Flag," *Harper's New Monthly Magazine* 26 (April 1863): 668–70.

7. David A. Wasson, "Shall We Compromise?" *Atlantic Monthly* 11 (May 1863): 651.

8. Charles Francis Adams, Jr., to father, November 18, 1864, *A Cycle of Adams Letters, 1861–1865*, vol. 2, ed. Worthington Chauncey Ford (Boston: Houghton Mifflin, 1920), 225; response to a serenade, November 10, 1864, *The Collected Works of Abraham Lincoln*, vol. 8, ed. Roy P. Basler (New Brunswick, N.J.: Rutgers University Press, 1953), 101; diary entry of November 16, 1864, *Lincoln and the Civil War in the Diaries and Letters of John Hay*, ed. Tyler Dennett (New York: Dodd, Mead, 1939), 242.

9. Thomas James Owen to father, mother, sister, April 16, 1865, *"Dear Friends at Home . . .",* 83.

10. Francis A. Riddle, "The Soldier's Place in Civilization," in *Military Essays and Recollections: Papers Read Before the Commandery of the State of Illinois, Military Order of the Loyal Legion of the United States*, vol. 2 (Chicago: A. C. McClurg, 1894), 515–17.

11. James Freeman Clarke article, quoted in *James Freeman Clarke: Autobiography, Diary and Correspondence*, ed. Edward Everett Hale (1891; reprint, New York: Negro Universities Press, 1968), 278.

12. Francis A. Lord, *They Fought for the Union* (Harrisburg, Pennsylvania: Stackpole, 1960), 1–17; Jacob Dolson Cox, *Military Reminiscences of the Civil War*, vol. 1 (New York: Charles Scribner's Sons, 1900), 166.

13. Jacob D. Cox, "War Preparations in the North," in *Battles and Leaders of the Civil War*, vol. 1, eds. Robert Underwood Johnson and Clarence Clough Buel (New York: Thomas Yoseloff, 1956), 94.

14. Frederick Pettit to sister, October 9, 1862, Pettit Papers, *Civil War Times Illustrated* Collection, U.S. Army Military History Institute.

15. Thomas Williams to Mrs. M. N. Williams, July 26, 1862, "Letters of General Thomas Williams, 1862," ed. G. Mott Williams, *American Historical Review* 14, no. 2 (January 1909): 327–28; George F. Williams, "Lights and Shadows of Army Life," *Century* 28, no. 6 (October 1884): 804.

16. Diary entry of October 29, 1862, *A Diary of Battle: The Personal Journals of Colonel Charles S. Wainwright, 1861–1865*, ed. Allan Nevins (New York: Harcourt, Brace and World, 1962), 117; Wainwright diary, August 9, 1863, ibid., 273; Thomas Wentworth Higginson, "Regular and Volunteer Officers," *Atlantic Monthly* 14 (September 1864): 351, 355.

17. Wilder Dwight to mother, September 7, 1861, *Life and Letters*, 97.

18. Eben P. Sturges to folks, June 9, 1864, *Civil War Times Illustrated* Collection, U.S. Army Military History Institute; Thomas Wentworth Higginson, "Regular and Volunteer Officers," 349.

19. Charles H. Brush to William E. Brush, August 25, 1862, Brush Family Papers, Illinois State Historical Library; Will C. Robinson to Mose, March 12, 1863, Robinson Papers, Illinois State Historical Library.

20. Ira Seymour Dodd, "The Household of the Hundred Thousand," in *The Song of the Rappahannock: Sketches of the Civil War* (New York: Dodd, Mead, 1898), 101; Jacob Dolson Cox, *Military Reminiscences of the Civil War*, vol. 1. 170.

21. *New York Times*, July 20, 1863; Nathan B. Webb diary, December 17, 1862, Illinois State Historical Library.

22. Tecumseh Steece, *A Republican Military System* (New York: John A. Gray & Green, 1863), 12–15, 25–26, 28–29; Ralph Waldo Emerson to Edward Waldo Emerson, ca. May 1864, *The Letters of Ralph Waldo Emerson*, vol. 5, ed. Ralph L. Rusk (New York: Columbia University Press, 1939), 378–79. Other commentators with the same idea as Steece included Henry Lee, *The Militia of the United States: What It Has Been: What It Should Be* (Boston: T. R. Marvin, 1864), 105–30; Charles Astor Bristed, "The Probable Influence of the New Military Element in Our Social and National Character," *United States Service Magazine* 1 (June 1864): 594, 598–601.

23. Henry F. Lyster, "Recollections of the Bull Run Campaign After Twenty-Seven Years," *A Paper Read Before Michigan Commandery of the Military Order of the Loyal Legion of the United States, February 1, 1887* (Detroit: William S. Ostler, 1888), 17; Ira Seymour Dodd, "The Making of a Regiment," *McClure's Magazine* 9 (1897): 1033.

24. Thomas L. Livermore, "The Northern Volunteers," *Journal of the Military Service Institution of the United States* 12 (September 1891): 914–16; Thomas Wentworth Higginson, "Regular and Volunteer Officers," 350; Ira Seymour Dodd, "The Making of a Regiment," 1034; Walter Carter to unidentified, May or June 1864, *Four Brothers in Blue: Or, Sunshine and Shadows of the War of the Rebellion* (1913; reprint, Austin: University of Texas Press, 1978), 411.

25. George P. Metcalf memoir, p. 70, Harrisburg Civil War Round Table–Gregory Coco Collection, U.S. Army Military History Institute; Ira Seymour Dodd, "The Making of a Regiment," 1033; Abner R. Small, *The Road to Richmond*, ed. Harold Adams Small (Berkeley: University of California Press, 1939), 193; Ira Seymour Dodd, "A Little Battle," in *Song of the Rappahannock*, 151.

26. Charles Edwards Lester, *Light and Dark of the Rebellion* (Philadelphia: George W. Childs, 1863), 9, 10; Henry T. Tuckerman, *The Rebellion: Its Latent Causes and True Significance* (New York: James G. Gregory, 1861), 8; Jane Grey Swisshelm to *St. Cloud Democrat*, July 2, 1863, *Crusader and Feminist: Letters of Jane Grey Swisshelm, 1858–1865*, ed. Arthur J. Larsen (St. Paul: Minnesota Historical Society, 1934), 236.

27. Maria Lydig Daly diary, July 28, 1861, *Diary of a Union Lady, 1861–1865*, ed. Harold Earl Hancock (New York: Funk and Wagnalls, 1962), 41; *New York Times*, August 17, 1862; Robert Hubbard to Nellie, May 21, 1863, Hubbard Papers, U.S.

Army Military History Institute; Walter Stone Poor to George Fox, July 25, 1862, "A Yankee Soldier in a New York Regiment," ed. James J. Heslin, *New-York Historical Society Quarterly* 50, no. 2 (April 1966): 130; Joseph Harrington Trego diary, April 20, 1861, Kansas State Historical Society.

28. Lydia Maria Child to William P. Cutler, July 10, 1862, *Lydia Maria Child: Selected Letters, 1817–1880*, eds. Milton Meltzer and Patricia G. Holland (Amherst: University of Massachusetts Press, 1982), 413; Lydia Maria Child to Sarah Shaw, October 30, 1862, *Child Letters*, 419.

29. Henry H. Smith diary, January 16, 1863, Illinois State Historical Library.

30. Thomas M. Covert to wife, September 21, 1862, Covert Papers, U.S. Army Military History Institute; Daniel Bond reminiscences, pp. 23–24, Minnesota Historical Society.

31. Ralph Waldo Emerson to James Elliot Cabot, August 4, 1861, *Emerson Letters*, vol. 5, 253; entry in 1862 journal, *Emerson Journals and Notebooks*, vol. 15, 208.

32. Walt Whitman to William D. O'Connor, September 11, 1864, *Walt Whitman: The Correspondence, Volume 1, 1842–1867*, ed. Edwin Haviland Miller (New York: New York University Press, 1961), 242; Whitman to Lewis K. Brown, November 9, 1863, ibid., 180; Whitman to Charles W. Eldridge, November 17, 1863, ibid., 185; James A. Connolly to Mary, August 21, 1864, *Three Years in the Army of the Cumberland: The Letters and Diary of James A. Connolly*, ed. Paul M. Angle (Bloomington: Indiana University Press, 1959), 256.

33. Horace James, *The Two Great Wars of America* (Boston: W. F. Brown, 1862), 11, 12.

34. Henry S. Olcott, "The War's Carnival of Fraud," in *Annals of the War Written by Leading Participants of North and South* (Philadelphia: Times, 1879), 706–07, 717, 723. See also Charles Leib, *Nine Months in the Quartermaster's Department; Or, The Chances for Making a Million* (Cincinnati: Moore, Wilstach, Keys, 1862).

35. Frederick Francis Cook, *Bygone Days in Chicago* (Chicago: A. C. McClurg, 1910), 130, 134–36, 160.

36. Jane Grey Swisshelm to *St. Cloud Democrat*, July 2, 1863, *Crusader and Feminist*, 237.

37. Oliver Wendell Holmes, Sr., "Bread and the Newspaper," in *The Complete Writings of Oliver Wendell Holmes*, vol. 8 (Boston: Houghton Mifflin, 1899), 8–10.

38. Ralph Waldo Emerson to Matilda Ashurst Biggs, April 8, 1863, *Emerson Letters*, vol. 5, 322; Arthur B. Carpenter to parents, April 11, 1861, quoted in Thomas R. Bright, "Yankees in Arms: The Civil War as a Personal Experience," *Civil War History* 19, no. 3 (September 1973): 199.

39. Jonathan P. Stowe to friends, June 18, 1862, *Civil War Times Illustrated* Collection, U.S. Army Military History Institute; Ralph Waldo Emerson to James Elliot Cabot, August 4, 1861, *Emerson Letters*, vol. 5, 253; Oliver Wendell Holmes, Sr., "Bread and the Newspaper," 14–15.

40. Alexis de Tocqueville, *Democracy in America*, vol. 2 (1835; reprint, New York: Alfred A. Knopf, 1980), 278.

41. Entry in 1863 journal, *Emerson Journals and Notebooks*, vol. 15, 351; entry in 1864–1865 journal, ibid., 163; Charles Russell Lowell to Josephine, September 10, 1863, *Life and Letters*, 301.

42. Oliver Wendell Holmes, Sr., to John Lothrop Motley, October 10, 1865, *The [Motley] Correspondence*, vol. 3 (New York: Harper and Brothers, 1900), 87–88; Lydia

Maria Child to Eliza Scudder, April 22, 1864, *Selected Letters*, 444; Charles Eliot Norton to G. W. Curtis, September 3, 1863, *Letters of Charles Eliot Norton*, vol. 1 (Boston: Houghton Miffin, 1913), 263.

43. Sanford Truesdell to Mrs. C. A. Merrill, July 31, 1862, Truesdell Papers, Joseph Regenstein Library, University of Chicago; Thomas Wentworth Higginson to James Freeman Clarke, November 5, 1861, *Letters and Journals of Thomas Wentworth Higginson, 1846–1906*, ed. Mary Thacher Higginson (1921, reprint, New York: Da Capa Press, 1969), 162; Charles Eliot Norton, "The Advantages of Defeat," *Atlantic Monthly* 8 (September 1861): 363.

44. Minor Milliken resolutions, quoted in Lester J. Cappon, "The Soldier's Creed," *Ohio Historical Quarterly* 64, no. 3 (July 1955): 327; Nadine Turchin diary, November 12, 1863, " 'A Monotony Full of Sadness:' The Diary of Nadine Turchin, May, 1863–April, 1864," ed. Mary Ellen McElligott, *Journal of the Illinois State Historical Society* 70, no. 1 (February 1977): 75; Walt Whitman to James P. Kirkwood, April 27(?), 1864, in *The Correspondence*, vol. 1, 214; E. H. Conger, "The Private," in *War Sketches and Incidents, Iowa Commandery, Military Order of the Loyal Legion of the United States*, vol. 2 (Des Moines, Iowa: Kenyon, 1898), 59.

45. "A Few Plain Words With the Rank and File of the Union Armies," in *Union Pamphlets of the Civil War, 1861–1865*, vol. 2, ed. Frank Freidel (Cambridge, Mass.: Harvard University Press, 1967), 1028–29; Charles Mackenzie, "The Great American Civil War," in *War Sketches and Incidents, Iowa Commandery, Military Order of the Loyal Legion of the United States*, vol. 1 (Des Moines, Iowa: P. C. Kenyon, 1893), 359.

46. Eudora Clark, "Hospital Memories," *Atlantic Monthly* 20 (September 1867): 330; Elvira J. Powers, *Hospital Pencillings: Being a Diary While in Jefferson General Hospital, Jeffersonville, Ind., and Others at Nashville, Tennessee* (Boston: Edward L. Mitchell, 1866), 22; entry of July 10, 1863, "The Civil War Diaries of Anna M. Ferris," ed. Harold B. Hancock, *Delaware History* 9, no. 3 (April 1961): 246.

47. Montgomery Schuyler Woodruff reminiscences, "The Civil War Notebook of Montgomery Schuyler Woodruff," ed. Frederick M. Woodruff, *Missouri Historical Society Bulletin* 29, no. 3 (April 1973): 188.

48. Charles Francis Adams, Jr., to father, May 24, 1863, *A Cycle of Adams Letters*, vol. 2, 14.

49. Minor Milliken resolutions, quoted in "The Soldier's Creed," 326–27; reply to New York Workingmen's Democratic Republican Association, March 21, 1864, *Collected Works of Lincoln*, vol. 7, 259; Robert C. Ogden to John E. Hart, June 8, 1863, Hart Papers, *Civil War Times Illustrated* Collection, U.S. Army Military History Institute; Thomas Wentworth Higginson to mother, January 29, 1862, *Letters and Journals*, 165.

50. Whitelaw Reid dispatch to *Cincinnati Gazette*, September 10, 1862, in *A Radical View: The 'Agate' Dispatches of Whitelaw Reid, 1861–1865*, vol. 1, ed. James G. Smart (Memphis: Memphis State University Press, 1976), 228; Oliver Wendell Holmes, Sr., "The Wormwood Cordial of History: With a Fable," *Atlantic Monthly* 8 (October 1861): 509–10; Lincoln to Joseph Hooker, January 26, 1863, *Collected Works of Lincoln*, vol. 6, 78–79.

51. Luther C. Furst diary, May 19, 1862, Harrisburg Civil War Round Table Collection, U.S. Army Military History Institute; Levi Adolphus Ross diary, July 1, 1863, Illinois State Historical Library; John Y. Foster, "Four Days at Gettysburg," *Harper's New Monthly Magazine* 28 (February 1864): 386–88.

52. Charles Dewolf journal, December 9, 1862, "A Yankee Cavalryman Views the

Battle of Prairie Grove: The Splendors and Horrors of a Battlefield," ed. Howard N. Monnett, *Arkansas Historical Quarterly* 21, no. 4 (Winter 1962): 301; Henry Dwight, "The War Album of Henry Dwight, Part II," ed. Albert Castel, *Civil War Times Illustrated* 19, no. 1 (April 1980): 24; John Burrill to parents, December 28, 1863, Burrill Papers, *Civil War Times Illustrated* Collection, U.S. Army Military History Institute; John Y. Foster, "Four Days at Gettysburg," 385; Harvey Reid to mother, April 24, 1863, *The View from Headquarters: Civil War Letters of Harvey Reid*, ed. Frank L. Byrne (Madison: State Historical Society of Wisconsin, 1965), 43; Reid to sisters, April 24, 1863, ibid., 43–44.

53. Theodore Lyman to wife, July 10, 1864, *Meade's Headquarters, 1863–1865: Letters of Colonel Theodore Lyman from the Wilderness to Appomattox*, ed. George R. Agassiz (Boston: Atlantic Monthly, 1922), 187.

54. Message to Congress in Special Session, July 4, 1861, *Collected Works of Lincoln*, vol. 4, 438; *Chicago Daily Journal*, April 17, 1861, in Northern Editorials on Secession, vol. 2, ed. Howard Cecil Perkins (New York: D. Appleton, 1942), 809.

55. Decimus et Ultimus Barziza, *The Adventures of a Prisoner of War, 1863–1864*, ed. R. Henderson Shuffler (1865; reprint, Austin: University of Texas Press, 1964), 59–61; Francis Wayland, Jr., "Letter to a Peace Democrat," *Atlantic Monthly* 12 (December 1863): 776; Joshua Lawrence Chamberlain, *The Passing of the Armies* (New York: G. P. Putnam's Sons, 1915), 12.

5. White Dissent, Black Freedom

1. *New York Times*, May 10, 1861, in *Northern Editorials on Secession*, vol. 2, ed. Howard Cecil Perkins (New York: D. Appleton, 1942), 833; note to a memo by Bates, April 15, 1861, *The Diary of Edward Bates, 1859–1866*, ed. Howard K. Beale (Washington, D.C.: Government Printing Office, 1933), 183; J. Randolph McBride to Lucas, August 5, 1861, McBride Papers, Indiana Historical Society.

2. Joseph L. Harsh, "George Brinton McClellan and the Forgotten Alternative: An Introduction to the Conservative Strategy in the Civil War: April–August 1861," (Ph.D. diss., Rice University, 1970), 43, 63, 73, 84–85, 195, 205; Rowena Reed, *Combined Operations in the Civil War* (Annapolis: Naval Institute Press, 1978), 36–39.

3. Herman Hattaway and Archer Jones, *How the North Won: A Military History of the Civil War* (Urbana: University of Illinois Press, 1983), 1–236.

4. Proclamation Suspending the Writ of Habeas Corpus, September 24, 1862, *The Collected Works of Abraham Lincoln*, vol. 5, ed. Roy P. Basler (New Brunswick, N.J.: Rutgers University Press, 1953), 436–37; John A. Marshall, *American Bastile: A History of the Illegal Arrests and Imprisonment of American Citizens During the Late Civil War* (1869; reprint, New York: Da Capo, 1970), 724.

5. Second Confiscation Act, July 17, 1862, *Congressional Globe*, 37th Congress, 2nd Session (Washington, D.C.: Globe, 1862), 412–13; First Confiscation Act, August 6, 1861, *Statutes at Large*, vol. 12 (Boston: Little, Brown, 1863), 319. The best study of confiscation is in John Syrett's "The Confiscation Acts; Efforts at Reconstruction during the Civil War" (Ph.D. diss., University of Wisconsin, 1971).

6. Preliminary Emancipation Proclamation, September 22, 1862, *Lincoln Works*, vol. 5, 433–36.

7. Eugene C. Murdock, *One Million Men: The Civil War Draft in the North* (Madison: State Historical Society of Wisconsin, 1971), 3–8.

8. Richard O. Curry, "The Union as It Was: A Critique of Recent Interpretations of the Copperheads," *Civil War History* 13, no. 1 (March 1967): 25–39; Nicholas B. Wainwright, "The Loyal Opposition in Civil War Philadelphia," *Pennsylvania Magazine of History and Biography* 88, no. 3 (July 1964): 294–315.

9. Lambdin P. Milligan speech, August 13, 1864, "Lambdin P. Milligan's Appeal for State's Rights," ed. Darwin Kelley, *Indiana Magazine of History* 66, no. 3 (September 1970): 281–82; Alexander Long speech, April 8, 1864, *Congressional Globe*, 38th Congress, 1st Session (Washington, D.C.: Globe, 1864), 1502.

10. John J. Davis to Anna Kennedy, June 1, 1862, "Ideology and Perception: Democratic and Republican Attitudes on Civil War Politics and the Statehood Movement in West Virginia," ed. Richard O. Curry, *West Virginia History* 44, no. 2 (Winter 1983): 144; Charles G. Wintersmith to Horatio Seymour, February 23, 1863, Wintersmith Papers, Illinois State Historical Library; Orasmas Elliott Niles to father, October 29, 1864, "Copperhead and Unionist: An Ex-Vermonter Tells His Father Why He Opposes the Civil War," *Vermont History* 41, no. 1 (Winter 1973): 3–5.

11. John M. Stucky to Lizzie, May 13, 1862, Stucky Papers, Indiana Historical Society; Eugene A. Carr to father, January 28, 1862, Carr Papers, U.S. Army Military History Institute.

12. Joanna D. Cowden, "The Politics of Dissent: Civil War Democrats in Connecticut," *New England Quarterly* 56, no. 4 (December 1983): 552; Joseph George, Jr., " 'Abraham Africanus I': President Lincoln Through the Eyes of a Copperhead Editor," *Civil War History* 14, no. 3 (September 1968): 232; H. H. Wubben, "Copperhead Charles Mason: A Question of Loyalty," *Civil War History* 24, no. 1 (March 1978): 48.

13. Jean H. Baker, *Affairs of Party: The Political Culture of Northern Democrats in the Mid-Nineteenth Century* (Ithaca: Cornell University Press, 1983), 153.

14. Ibid., 155–157.

15. *Wheeling Register*, October 12, 1863, "Ideology and Perception," 145; John A. Marshall, *American Bastile*, xxvii, xxxii; Joseph George, Jr., " 'A Catholic Family Newspaper' Views the Lincoln Administration: John Mullaly's Copperhead Weekly," *Civil War History* 24, no. 2 (June 1978): 112–32; Alfred A. Curtis to William R. Whittingham, July 18, 1863, "Bishop Whittingham, Mount Calvary Church, and the Battle of Gettysburg," ed. Edward N. Todd, *Maryland Historical Magazine* 60, no. 3 (September 1965): 326.

16. Entry of April 8, 1863, *A Virginia Yankee in the Civil War: The Diaries of David Hunter Strother*, ed. Cecil D. Eby, Jr. (Chapel Hill: University of North Carolina Press, 1961), 166; entry of September 27, 1863, *A Diary of Battle: The Personal Journals of Colonel Charles S. Wainwright, 1861–1865*, ed. Allan Nevins (New York: Harcourt, Brace and World, 1962), 283–84.

17. George Sheeks to cousin, May 2, 1863, Jonathan Turley Papers, Indiana State Library.

18. Jean H. Baker, *Affairs of Party*, 169; Garrett Davis speech, January 14, 1864, *Congressional Globe*, 38th Congress, 1st Session, 177.

19. Arnold M. Shankman, *The Pennsylvania Antiwar Movement, 1861–1865* (Rutherford, N.J.: Fairleigh Dickinson University Press, 1980), 14, 16–17, 217–19.

20. Seneca B. Thrall to wife, September 24, 1863, "An Iowa Doctor in Blue: The Letters of Seneca B. Thrall, 1862–1864," ed. Mildred Throne, *Iowa Journal of History*

58, no. 2 (April 1960): 169; Adolph Engelmann to sister, February 2, 1863, Engelmann-Kircher Collection, Illinois State Historical Library; Robert C. Ogden to John E. Hart, June 8, 1863, Hart Papers, *Civil War Times Illustrated* Collection, U.S. Army Military History Institute; Walt Whitman to Lewis K. Brown, November 8, 1863, *Walt Whitman: The Correspondence, Volume 1, 1842–1867*, ed. Edwin Haviland Miller (New York: New York University Press, 1961), 176.

21. Francis Wayland, Jr., "Letter to a Peace Democrat," *Atlantic Monthly* 12 (December 1863): 788; Sidney George Fisher diary, May 8, 1863, *A Philadelphia Perspective: The Diary of Sidney George Fisher Covering the Years 1834–1871*, ed. Nicholas B. Wainwright (Philadelphia: Historical Society of Pennsylvania, 1967), 451; entry of September 13, 1864, *The Diary of George Templeton Strong: The Civil War, 1860–1865*, ed. Allan Nevins and Milton Halsey Thomas (New York: Macmillan, 1952), 486.

22. James Weiler to Joseph P. Vannest, April 19, 1863, Vannest Papers, Indiana Historical Society; George B. Turner to mother, April 8, 1863, Turner Papers, Ohio Historical Society; Ezra Farnsworth, "At the Rear in War Times," in *Glimpses of the Nation's Struggle: Papers Read Before the Minnesota Commandery of the Military Order of the Loyal Legion of the United States, January, 1903–1908*, Sixth Series (Minneapolis: Aug. Davis, 1909), 410–11.

23. Jane Grey Swisshelm to *St. Cloud Democrat*, April 11, 1863, *Crusader and Feminist: Letters of Jane Grey Swisshelm, 1858–1865*, ed. Arthur J. Larsen (Saint Paul: Minnesota Historical Society, 1934), 212.

24. In addition to newspapers, Funk's speech was printed in "Copperheads Under the Heel of an Illinois Farmer," *Union Pamphlets of the Civil War, 1861–1865*, vol. 2, ed. Frank Freidel (Cambridge, Mass.: Harvard University Press, 1967), 607–10; Latitia Moody to Funk, February 18, 1863, Funk Papers, Illinois State Historical Library; Jonathan B. Turner to Funk, February 20, 1863, ibid. The Funk papers contain about thirty letters in regard to his speech; all are praiseworthy.

25. Alexander B. Cooper, "Alexander B. Cooper's Civil War Memories of Camden," ed. Harold B. Hancock, *Delaware History* 20, no. 1 (Spring-Summer 1982): 62; Horace M. Brown, "A Small Boy's Recollections of the War Time," in *War Papers Read Before the Commandery of the State of Wisconsin, Military Order of the Loyal Legion of the United States, Volume 3* (Milwaukee: Burdick and Allen, 1903), 210.

26. Thomas H. Smith, "Crawford County 'Ez Trooly Dimecratic': A Study of Midwestern Copperheadism," *Ohio History* 76, nos. 1 and 2 (Winter and Spring 1967): 33–53; John E. Talmadge, "A Peace Movement in Civil War Connecticut," *New England Quarterly* 37, no. 3 (September 1964): 306–21; Frank Freidel, "The Loyal Publication Society: A Pro-Union Propaganda Agency," *Mississippi Valley Historical Review* 26, no. 3 (December 1939): 359–64; George P. Metcalf memoir, 163–64, Harrisburg Civil War Round Table-Gregory Coco Collection, U.S. Army Military History Institute; Frank L. Klement, *The Copperheads in the Middle West* (Chicago: University of Chicago Press, 1960), 206–26.

27. Craig D. Tenney, "To Suppress or Not to Suppress: Abraham Lincoln and the Chicago *Times*," *Civil War History* 27, no. 3 (September 1981): 248–59; Sidney George Fisher diary, April 15, 1865, *A Philadelphia Perspective*, 493.

28. Francis Wayland, Jr., "Letter to a Peace Democrat," 782.

29. Joel H. Silbey, *A Respectable Minority: The Democratic Party in the Civil War Era, 1860–1868* (New York: W. W. Norton, 1977), 115–39; James K. Newton to mother, November 9, 1864, *A Wisconsin Boy in Dixie: The Selected Letters of James K. Newton*, ed. Stephen E. Ambrose (Madison: University of Wisconsin Press, 1961), 128; Hugh C.

Perkins to friend, October 16, 1864, Harrisburg Civil War Round Table Collection, U.S. Army Military History Institute; Will C. Robinson to Charlie, August 25, 1864, Robinson Papers, Illinois State Historical Library.

30. Henry Winter Davis speech, November 1861, in *Speeches and Addresses* (New York: Harper and Brothers, 1867), 290–91.

31. Entry in 1862 journal, *The Journals and Miscellaneous Notebooks of Ralph Waldo Emerson*, vol. 15, ed. Linda Allardt (Cambridge, Mass.: Harvard University Press, 1982), 209.

32. Diary entry of January 1, 1862, *Diary & Letters of Rutherford Birchard Hayes*, vol. 2, ed. Charles Richard Williams (Columbus: Ohio State Archaeological and Historical Society, 1922), 173–74.

33. Robert H. Earnest to James, November 17, 1862, Earnest Papers, Kentucky Historical Society; Orestes Augustus Brownson, "Brownson on the Rebellion," in *Union Pamphlets of the Civil War*, vol. 1, 153.

34. Lydia Maria Child to George W. Julian, January 30, 1862, *Lydia Maria Child: Selected Letters, 1817–1880*, eds. Milton Meltzer and Patricia G. Holland (Amherst: University of Massachusetts Press, 1982), 403; J. T. Trowbridge, "We Are a Nation," *Atlantic Monthly* 14 (December 1864): 773; Abraham Lincoln to Albert G. Hodges, April 4, 1864, *Collected Works*, vol. 7, 281.

35. Richard Busteed speech, August 27, 1862, *New York Times*, August 28, 1862; Harvey Reid to father, September 19, 1863, *The View from Headquarters: Civil War Letters of Harvey Reid*, ed. Frank L. Byrne (Madison: State Historical Society of Wisconsin, 1965), 91.

36. Marc W. Kruman, "Dissent in the Confederacy: The North Carolina Experience," *Civil War History* 27, no. 4 (December 1981): 294–95, 297–311; Eric L. McKitrick, "Party Politics and the Union and Confederate War Efforts," in *The American Party Systems: Stages of Political Development*, eds. William Nisbet Chambers and Walter Dean Burnham (New York: Oxford University Press, 1967), 120–21, 145–46.

37. Jean H. Baker, *Affairs of Party*, 175–76.

38. John Russell to sister, July 16, 1862, Russell Papers, *Civil War Times Illustrated* Collection, U.S. Army Military History Institute; Jasper Barney to brother, October 24, 1862, John C. Dinsmore Papers, Illinois State Historical Library; Henry Martyn Cross to parents, January 11, 1863, "A Yankee Soldier Looks at the Negro," 136.

39. Charles Francis Adams, Jr., to father, July 23, 1861, *A Cycle of Adams Letters, 1861–1865*, vol. 1, ed. Worthington Chauncey Ford (Boston: Houghton Mifflin, 1920), 23; Thomas Wentworth Higginson to mother, February 21, 1862, *Letters and Journals of Thomas Wentworth Higginson, 1846–1906*, ed. Mary Thacher Higginson (1921; reprint, New York: Da Capo Press, 1969), 166; John Russell to sister, February 26, 1863, Russell Papers, *Civil War Times Illustrated* Collection, U.S. Army Military History Institute.

40. Entry of August 19, 1864, *The Diary of George Templeton Strong: The Civil War*, 474; Charles Francis Adams, Jr., to father, July 16, 1862, *A Cycle of Adams Letters*, vol. 1, 165; Charles Francis Adams, Jr., to Henry Adams, July 28, 1862, ibid., vol. 1, 172.

41. Sidney George Fisher diary, October 27, 1863, *A Philadelphia Perspective*, 462; James A. Connolly to wife, November 22, 1863, *Three Years in the Army of the Cumberland: The Letters and Diary of James A. Connolly*, ed. Paul M. Angle (Bloomington: Indiana University Press, 1959), 146; Mary J. Anderson to James Nesbitt, December 8, 1862, Nesbitt-Raub Papers, U.S. Army Military History Institute.

42. Lydia Maria Child to Mary Stearns, December 22, 1862, *Child Letters*, 422.

43. George H. Barker to James Miner, September 16, 1861, Miner Family Papers, Illinois State Historical Library; John Burrill to parents, November 7, 1863, Burrill Papers, *Civil War Times Illustrated* Collection, U.S. Army Military History Institute; Oliver Edwards, "My Recollections of the Civil War," p. 46, Illinois State Historical Library; John Russell to sister, May 1, 1863, Russell Papers, *Civil War Times Illustrated* Collection, U.S. Army Military History Institute.

44. Benjamin Stevens to mother, August 12, 1863, "The Civil War Letters of an Iowa Family," ed. Richard N. Ellis, *Annals of Iowa* 39, no. 8 (Spring 1969): 582; Henry Martyn Cross to parents, May 4, 1863, "A Yankee Soldier Looks at the Negro," 144; James A. Connolly diary, November 20, 1864, *Three Years in the Army of the Cumberland*, 313.

45. John Murray Forbes to Gustavus Vasa Fox, September 6, 1864, *Letters and Recollections*, vol. 2, ed. Sarah Forbes Hughes (Boston: Houghton Mifflin, 1900), 104.

46. Jacob Behm to brother and sister, February 18, 1863, *Civil War Times Illustrated* Collection, U.S. Army Military History Institute.

47. Henry Martyn Cross to parents, January 11, 1863, "A Yankee Soldier Looks at the Negro," 136; Frederick Pettit to parents, brothers, and sisters, March 12, 1863, *Civil War Times Illustrated* Collection, U.S. Army Military History Institute.

6. Continuity and Change

1. William W. Averell memoir, p. 2, Lewis Leigh Collection, U.S. Army Military History Institute; Albion W. Tourgee, *The Story of a Thousand* (Buffalo: S. McGerald, 1896), 17.

2. Henry A. Barnum oration, *Society of the Army of the Cumberland, Fifth Re-Union, Detroit, 1871* (Cincinnati: Robert Clarke, 1872), 58–59; Jasper P. George autobiography, pp. 1–3, Civil War Miscellaneous Collection, U.S. Army Military History Institute; George H. Corey, *Wisdom and War: A Discourse . . . Delivered Before the Department of the Potomac, Grand Army of the Republic* (Washington: Gibson Brothers, 1889), 14–15; Stuart Taylor oration, *The Society of the Army of the Potomac: Report of the Seventeenth Annual Re-Union at San Francisco, August 2nd and 4th, 1886* (New York: MacGowan and Slipper, 1886), 35; Albion W. Tourgee, *The Veteran and His Pipe* (Chicago: Belford, Clarke, 1888), 10.

3. Edwin Lewis Suter, "The New Republic," *Blue and Gray* 1, no. 6 (June 1893): 441–42; Gates P. Thruston oration, *Society of the Army of the Cumberland, Twenty-First Reunion, Toledo, Ohio, 1890* (Cincinnati: Robert Clarke, 1891), 126.

4. John B. Sanborn, "Remarks of Past Commander John B. Sanborn, Transferring the Commandery to Commander General William R. Marshall," in *Glimpses of the Nation's Struggle: A Series of Papers Read Before the Minnesota Commandery of the Military Order of the Loyal Legion of the United States*, First Series (St. Paul, Minn.: St. Paul Book and Stationery, 1887), 411–12; John H. Martindale address, *Society of the Army of the Potomac: Record of Proceedings at the Second Annual Re-Union, Held in the City of Philadelphia, April 9th, 1870* (New York: Crocker Brothers, 1871), 9; C. A. Boutelle remarks, *First Maine Bugle* Campaign 2, Call 2 (October 1890): 30.

5. Henry Ward Beecher speech, April 14, 1865, in Franklin Jordan, "The Occupation of Fort Sumter and Hoisting the Old Flag," *A Paper Prepared and Read Before California Commandery of the Military Order of the Loyal Legion of the United States, October 7, 1896*

(N.p., n.d.), 24; Henry Winter Davis oration, July 4, 1865, in *Speeches and Addresses* (New York: Harper and Brothers, 1867), 570–71.

6. Regis de Trobriand, *Four Years with the Army of the Potomac* (1867; English ed., Boston: Ticknor, 1889), 3; Thomas F. Barr, "Costs and Compensations of the War," in *Military Essays and Recollections: Papers Read Before the Commandery of the State of Illinois, Military Order of the Loyal Legion of the United States*, vol. 1 (Chicago: A. C. McClurg, 1891), 520; George H. Corey, *Wisdom and War*, 14.

7. Henry Ward Beecher speech, April 14, 1865, in Franklin Jordan, "The Occupation of Fort Sumter," 23; Rutherford B. Hayes remarks, *Report of the Proceedings of the Society of the Army of the Tennessee at the Fourteenth Annual Meeting, Held at Cincinnati, Ohio, April 6th and 7th, 1881* (Cincinnati: The Society of the Army of the Tennessee, 1885), 135.

8. Michael J. Brodhead, "Accepting the Verdict: National Supremacy as Expressed in State Constitutions, 1861–1912," *Nevada Historical Society Quarterly* 13, no. 2 (Summer 1970): 3–16; Henry Ward Beecher speech, April 14, 1865, in Franklin Jordan, "The Occupation of Fort Sumter," 12.

9. Nixon B. Stewart, *Dan McCook's Regiment, 52nd O.V.I.* (Alliance, Ohio: Review, 1900), 10; George H. Corey, *Wisdom and War*, 15.

10. R. L. Ashhurst, *Address to the Survivors' Association of the 150th Regiment, Pennsylvania Volunteers* (Philadelphia: Allen, Lane, and Scott, 1896), 9–10; Buren R. Sherman, "The Legacy of the War," in *War Sketches and Incidents, Iowa Commandery, Military Order of the Loyal Legion of the United States*, vol. 2 (Des Moines, Iowa: Kenyon, 1898), 84.

11. W. G. Veazey address, *Proceedings of the Reunion Society of Vermont Officers*, 1864–1884 (Burlington, Vt.: Free Press Association, 1885), 47–48; Lucius Bigelow oration, ibid., 294; Henry Ward Beecher oration, *Society of the Army of the Potomac: Report of the Ninth Annual Re-Union, at Springfield, Mass., June 5, 1878* (New York: MacGowan and Slipper, 1878), 23.

12. Michael H. Fitch, *Echoes of the Civil War As I Hear Them* (New York: R. F. Fenno, 1905), 347–48; Arthur Little oration, *The Society of the Army of the Potomac: Report of the Twenty-fourth Annual Re-Union at Boston, Mass., June 27th and 28th, 1893* (New York: MacGowan and Slipper, 1893), 33.

13. Carl A. G. Adae, "Our Military Future," in *Sketches of War History, 1861–1865: Papers Read Before the Ohio Commandery of the Military Order of the Loyal Legion of the United States, 1883–1886*, vol. 1 (Cincinnati: Robert Clarke, 1888), 328; John W. Deforest, "Our Military Past and Present," *Atlantic Monthly* 44 (November 1879): 572; Thomas Wentworth Higginson, "Our Future Militia System," *Atlantic Monthly* 16 (September 1865); 371–78; John A. Logan, *The Volunteer Soldier of America* (Chicago: R. S. Peale, 1887), 78, 457, 605–06.

14. Charles Royster, *A Revolutionary People at War: The Continental Army and American Character, 1775–1783* (New York: W. W. Norton, 1979), 178, 295–330, 368.

15. I. P. Powell, "Address," in *War Papers Read Before the Michigan Commandery of the Military Order of the Loyal Legion of the United States*, vol. 2, (Detroit: James H. Stone, 1898), 322; W. G. Veazey address, *Proceedings of the Reunion Society of Vermont Officers*, 47.

16. William H. Vilas speech, *Report of the Proceedings of the Society of the Army of the Tennessee at the Twelfth Annual Meeting Held at Indianapolis, Indiana, October 30th and 31st, 1878* (N.p., n.d.), 188; I. P. Powell, "Address," in *War Papers, Michigan MOLLUS*, vol. 2, 323.

17. John M. Palmer oration, *Society of the Army of the Cumberland, Fourth Re-Union*,

Cleveland, 1870, 49–50; Ulysses S. Grant, *Personal Memoirs*, vol. 2 (New York: Charles L. Webster, 1885), 544.

18. W. Q. Gresham address, *Report of the Proceedings of the Society of the Army of the Tennessee, at the Thirteenth Annual Meeting, Held at Chicago, Illinois, November 12th and 13th, 1879* (N.p., n.d.), 431; Charles A. Woodruff, "Our Boys in the War of the Rebellion," *A Paper Prepared and Read Before California Commandery of the Military Order of the Loyal Legion of the United States, November 12, 1890* (N.p., n.d.), 21; R. L. Ashhurst, *Address to the Survivors' Association*, 13–14, 19.

19. A. C. Voris, "The Battle of the Boys," in *Sketches of War History, 1861–1865: Papers Prepared for the Ohio Commandery of the Military Order of the Loyal Legion of the United States, 1890–1896*, vol. 4 (Cincinnati: Robert Clarke, 1896), 90; Thomas H. McKee, "Views and Reviews of the Civil War," in *War Papers, Military Order of the Loyal Legion of the United States, Commandery of the District of Columbia* (N.p., n.d.), 15.

20. Eugene M. Wilson, "The Blessings of War," *Glimpses of the Nation's Struggle, Minnesota MOLLUS*, First Series, 177; Joseph B. Peaks oration, *First Maine Cavalry Association: Record of Proceedings at the Tenth Annual Reunion, Held at Dover, 1881* (Augusta, Maine: Kennebec Journal, 1882), 19; Augustus L. Chetlain speech, *Report of the Proceedings of the Society of the Army of the Tennessee, at the Nineteenth Meeting, Held at Rock Island, Ill., September 15th and 16th, 1886* (N.p., n.d.), 356; Franklin M. Drew, "The Civil War," in *War Papers Read Before the Commandery of the State of Maine, Military Order of the Loyal Legion of the United States*, vol. 2 (Portland, Maine: Lefavor-Tower, 1902), 321; Nelson A. Miles, *Personal Recollections and Observations of General Nelson A. Miles* (Chicago: Warner, 1897), 49; Thomas H. McKee, "The Test of Loyalty in the State of Virginia in 1861," in *War Papers, Military Order of the Loyal Legion of the United States, Commandery of the District of Columbia* (N.p., n.d.), 11.

21. Edward W. Spangler, *My Little War Experience* (York, Pa.: York Daily, 1904), iii; George E. Sutherland, "The Negro in the Late War," in *War Papers Read Before the Commandery of the State of Wisconsin, Military Order of the Loyal Legion on the United States*, vol. 1 (Milwaukee: Burdick, Armitage and Allen, 1891), 187.

22. John M. Palmer oration, *Society of the Army of the Cumberland, Fourth Re-Union, Cleveland, 1870* (Cincinnati: Robert Clarke, 1870), 43–44; John A. Logan, *The Volunteer Soldier of America*, 85–86; James Russell Lowell, "Scotch the Snake, or Kill It?" in *The Complete Writings, Vol. 6, Political Essays* (Cambridge, Mass.: Riverside Press, 1904), 314.

23. Ulysses S. Grant, *Personal Memoirs*, vol. 2, 511–12; Henry Winter Davis oration, July 4, 1865, in *Speeches and Addresses*, 581–84; John A. Logan, *The Volunteer Soldier of America*, 380.

24. George H. Corey, *Wisdom and War*, 15–16; Rutherford B. Hayes remarks, *Report of Proceedings, Society of the Army of the Tennessee, Fourteenth Meeting, 1881*, 137.

25. Stanley Matthews oration, *Society of the Army of the Cumberland, Eighth Re-Union, Columbus, 1874* (Cincinnati: Robert Clarke, 1875), 77–78.

26. George H. Corey, *Wisdom and War*, 12; Augustus Buell, *"The Cannoneer": Recollections of Service in the Army of the Potomac* (Washington, D.C.: National Tribune, 1890), 104.

27. Ulysses S. Grant, *Personal Memoirs*, vol. 1, 221.

28. Edgar Holden, "The 'Sassacus' and the 'Albemarle,' " in *Personal Recollections of the War of the Rebellion: Addresses Delivered Before the New York Commandery of the Loyal Legion of the United States, 1883–1891* (New York: J. J. Little, 1891), 96; E. B. Parsons, "Missionary Ridge," in *War Papers Read Before the Commandery of the State of Wisconsin,*

Military Order of the Loyal Legion of the United States, vol. 1 (Milwaukee: Burdick, Armitage, and Allen, 1891), 189.

29. Charles A. Woodruff, "Our Boys in the War of the Rebellion," *California MOLLUS, November 12, 1890*, 3; George W. Burnell, "Our Grandfathers and Ourselves," in *War Papers Read Before the Commandery of the State of Wisconsin, Military Order of the Loyal Legion of the United States*, vol. 4 (Milwaukee: Burdick and Allen, 1914), 107, 118–19; Henry A. Barnum oration, *Society of the Army of the Cumberland, Fifth Re-Union, 1871*, 57–58.

30. Nathaniel Southgate Shaler, *The Citizen: A Study of the Individual and the Government* (Boston: Houghton Mifflin, 1904), 61; Rutherford B. Hayes remarks, *Report of Proceedings, Society of the Army of the Tennessee, Fourteenth Meeting, 1881*, 136.

31. Albion W. Tourgee, *An Appeal to Caesar*, 9–17.

32. Tourgee, *The Veteran and His Pipe*, 15–16.

33. Tourgee, *An Appeal to Caesar*, 56–58, 72, 153–54.

34. Tourgee, *The Veteran and His Pipe*, 166, 246–47.

35. Tourgee, *An Appeal to Caesar*, 44–49.

36. Ibid., 52, 127, 260–381.

37. Tourgee, *The Veteran and His Pipe*, 4; Joshua Chamberlain oration, *First Maine Cavalry Association: Record of Proceedings at the Eleventh Annual Reunion, Held at Brunswick, 1882* (Augusta, Maine: Kennebec Journal, 1885), 11–12.

38. John A. Logan, *The Great Conspiracy: Its Origin and History* (New York: A. R. Hart, 1886), 670; Nelson A. Miles, *Personal Recollections and Observations*, 49; Charles Anderson, "Major Robert Anderson at Fort Sumter," *Sketches of War History, Ohio MOLLUS*, vol. 4, 105.

39. Ralph Waldo Emerson, "The Fortune of the Republic," in *The Complete Works of Ralph Waldo Emerson*, vol. 11, ed. Edward Waldo Emerson (Boston: Houghton Mifflin, 1904), 511–44; Cruce Stark, "Brothers at/in War: One Phase of Post–Civil War Reconciliation," *Canadian Review of American Studies* 6, no. 2 (Fall 1975): 177–78.

40. Charles Robinson, "My Experience in the Civil War," *Michigan History Magazine* 24, no. 1 (Winter 1940): 50; Lucius Bigelow oration, *Proceedings of the Reunion Society of Vermont Officers, 1864–1884*, 290–92.

41. Jane Stuart Woolsey, *Hospital Days* (New York: D. Van Nostrand, 1870), 6; Carl A. G. Adae, "Our Military Future," *Sketches of War History, Ohio MOLLUS*, vol. 1, 315; Robert Goldthwaite Carter, *Four Brothers in Blue: Or, Sunshine and Shadows of the Rebellion* (1913; reprint, Austin: University of Texas Press, 1978), 2–3; Annie Wittenmyer, *Under the Guns: A Woman's Reminiscences of the Civil War* (Boston: E. B. Stillings, 1895), 270–71.

42. See "The Soldier's Faith," "Memorial Day," "Rudolph C. Lehmann," "Albert Venn Dicey," and "The Class of '61," all in *The Occasional Speeches of Justice Oliver Wendell Holmes*, comp. Mark DeWolfe Howe (Cambridge, Mass.: Harvard University Press, 1962).

43. Henry Ward Beecher oration, *Society of the Army of the Potomac, Report of Ninth Re-Union, 1878*, 28; John A. Logan, *The Volunteer Soldier of America*, 398.

44. Augustus L. Chetlain speech, *Report of the Proceedings, Society of the Army of the Tennessee, Nineteenth Meeting, 1886*, 357–61; Albion W. Tourgee, *Murvale Eastman, Christian Socialist* (New York: Fords, Howard and Hulbert, 1890), i–v.

45. Henry H. Sibley, "Letter of Past Commander Henry H. Sibley," in *Glimpses of the Nation's Struggle: A Series of Papers Read Before the Minnesota Commandery of the Military Order of the Loyal Legion of the United States, 1887–1889*, Second Series (St. Paul, Minn.: St. Paul Book and Stationery, 1890), 412; Albion W. Tourgee, *Murvale Eastman*, iv–v.

46. John Ireland remarks, *Report of the Proceedings of the Society of the Army of the Tennessee at the Thirty-Sixth Meeting, Held at Council Bluffs, Iowa, November 8–9, 1906*, (Cincinnati: Charles O. Nebel, 1907), 160–61.

47. Augustus L. Chetlain speech, *Report of the Proceedings, Society of the Army of the Tennessee, Nineteenth Meeting, 1886*, 361–62; Walter Q. Gresham address, *Report of the Proceedings, Society of the Army of the Tennessee, Thirteenth Meeting, 1879*, 342–44.

48. R. L. Ashhurst, *Address to the Survivors' Association*, 13–14; Nathaniel Wales, untitled paper, p. 1, Massachusetts MOLLUS Collection, U.S. Army Military History Institute.

49. My belief in the significance of change spurred by the coming of age of a new generation was influenced by Robert H. Wiebe, *The Search for Order, 1877–1920* (New York: Hill and Wang, 1967), 147.

50. William W. Averell memoir, pp. 1–2, Lewis Leigh Collection, U.S. Army Military History Institute; Alfred T. Andreas, "Woman and the Rebellion," in *Military Essays and Recollections: Papers Read Before the Commandery of the State of Illinois, Military Order of the Loyal Legion of the United States*, vol. 2 (Chicago: A. C. McClurg, 1894), 423–25.

51. John G. Cawelti, *Apostles of the Self-Made Man: Changing Concepts of Success in America* (Chicago: University of Chicago Press, 1965), 169–73, 180, 184–89.

52. Daniel Horowitz, *The Morality of Spending: Attitudes Toward the Consumer Society in America, 1875–1940* (Baltimore: Johns Hopkins University Press, 1985), xxi–xxxi.

53. The quote is from William R. Leach, "Transformations in a Culture of Consumption: Women and Department Stores, 1890–1925," *Journal of American History* 71, no. 2 (September 1984): 320; T. J. Jackson Lears, "From Salvation to Self-Realization: Advertising and the Therapeutic Roots of the Consumer Culture, 1880–1930," in *The Culture of Consumption: Critical Essays in American History, 1880–1980*, ed. Richard Wightman Fox and T. J. Jackson Lears (New York: Pantheon, 1983), 21, 34–35; David M. Potter, *People of Plenty: Economic Abundance and the American Character* (Chicago: University of Chicago Press, 1954), 169, 188.

54. Byron O. Carr to father, April 24, 1862, Eugene A. Carr Papers, U.S. Army Military History Institute.

Index